Two Balls or less

Two Balls or less

Jenny Hill

David and Charles

A DAVID & CHARLES BOOK
Copyright © David & Charles Limited 2007

David & Charles is an F+W Publications Inc. company
4700 East Galbraith Road
Cincinnati, OH 45236

First published in the UK in 2007

Text and designs copyright © Jenny Hill 2007
Photographs copyright © David and Charles 2007

A catalogue record for this book is available from the British Library.

ISBN-13: 978-0-7153-2431-8 paperback
ISBN-10: 0-7153-2431-4 paperback

Printed in China by SNP Leefung Pte Ltd
for David & Charles
Brunel House   Newton Abbot   Devon

Executive Editor Cheryl Brown
Desk Editor Bethany Dymond
Head of Design Prudence Rogers
Project Editor Nicola Hodgson
Production Controller Ros Napper
Photographer Lorna Yabsley

Visit our website at www.davidandcharles.co.uk

David & Charles books are available from all good bookshops; alternatively you can contact our Orderline on
0870 9908222 or write to us at FREEPOST EX2 110, D&C Direct, Newton Abbot, TQ12 4ZZ (no stamp required UK only);
US customers call 800-289-0963 and Canadian customers call 800-840-5220.

contents

introduction

This book celebrates the new generation of gorgeous gourmet yarns that are available to modern knitters and crocheters.

Visiting a yarn store used to be a straightforward experience. You could walk in, choose a weight of yarn to match the pattern you were planning to make, and then pick out a colour or three. Simple. Now there is a whole new dimension: texture. Not just texture as in 'a bit fluffy' or 'quite shiny', but something really different, from poke-your-eye-out wild, to yarn so alluringly soft and fluffy you want to bury your face in it (don't try this in the yarn store!).

It's goodbye to plain old wool and humdrum cotton and hello to a whole new world of tantalising treats: luxurious mixtures of cashmere and angora, slinky twists of ribbon, gauzy mixes of mohair and silk, loopy bubbly bouclé, sparkling lurex, lush alpaca, and tufty, shaggy yarns reminiscent of fleeces and fake fur. And then there's colour to play with… from beautifully subtle hand-dyed shades that melt and merge into one another, to outrageously bright and vibrant synthetics, exploring yarn through colour is a truly glorious experience.

This book features 20 inspiring projects, split across four categories: home, kids, adults, and gifts. And dedicated knitters should take a deep breath… each section includes one crochet design. If you haven't tried crochet yet, I promise that if you spend half an hour practising using the simple step-by-step instructions (see pages 22–23), you will be proficient enough to complete any of the crochet designs without yarn-related tears.

Every project in this book requires two balls…or less. Why two balls? Small-scale projects are ideal for experimenting with new types of yarn without worrying too much about the cost (and some designer yarns come with a hefty price tag). But don't begrudge the cost; if you are going to make something with just two balls, you may as well make sure they are beautiful, unique and just a little bit special.

Using one or two balls doesn't put a straitjacket on creativity: there are more fabulous designs that can be made with one or two balls than can fit into just one book, or indeed a whole bookstore. And these projects offer a significant advantage: they can be made quickly and simply. All the projects in this book are pretty straightforward; if you need extra support, refer to the techniques section (pages 16–21).

So, next time you take a trip to the yarn store, don't bypass the 'fancy' section; dive in and choose something different to explore and experiment with. I hope this book will guide you through the new world of gourmet yarns, giving advice on the yarns and how best to use them, and inspire you to slip a little luxury onto your needles.

adventures in yarn

In this section, we look at the tempting array of glorious gourmet yarns available, celebrating the properties that make them so special and giving advice on how best to show them off.

Caught by the fuzz: furry and fuzzy yarns

What is it?
Furry and fuzzy yarns are available with either a short pile or a longer pile of feathery strands. When knitted up, these yarns have a lush texture that can be light-weight with fronds, or shaggy and furry. They are available in both synthetic and natural fibres and a number of weights; the heavier yarns knit up to create a fairly dense fabric that resembles fake fur.

What can I make with it?
I used a mohair-and-wool mix fake-fur yarn to trim the crocheted baby bonnets (pages 46–49). I also used an extravagant concoction of synthetic fibres for the Bollywood bag (pages 106–108).

What's it for?
Fake-fur yarns are ideal for trimmings, such as collars and cuffs. They are beautiful when used in knits for the home; use them to make a luxurious caramel border for a cream cable-knit blanket, or to add a stripe of texture across the middle of an otherwise plain cushion. Furry, fuzzy yarns are also a great fabric for children.

Yarn hints and tips
It's best to use these yarns with simple stitches, as all stitch definition will be lost behind the tufts and fibres. Also, this yarn can be tricky to knit with because the individual stitches on the needle are hard to see. Pay close attention to what you're doing – work in a good light!

Furry and fuzzy yarns vary in thickness from feathery to shaggy; all are gloriously tactile.

Wild at heart: wild yarns

Wild yarns combine extravagant, exuberant texture featuring a mixture of fibres with a wild and heady approach to colour.

What is it?
Wild, crazy yarns are packed with personality. The construction of these yarns tends to feature a core thread, sometimes shot through with lurex, with other strands of fabric or straggles of rags flaring out at intervals to create a lively, dramatic effect. These yarns often feature both a mixture of textures and vibrant colours.

What can I make with it?
In this book, I've used a wild raggy-ribbon yarn to make a strikingly colourful storage cube (pages 34–37), and a fun, tufty yarn for a children's gilet (pages 64–66).

What's it for?
Wild yarns may seem quite childlike and garish when you see them on the shelf, but they can be used to make sophisticated items. They look amazing when worked up into larger garments such as cardigans, and make lively and colourful fashion accessories.

Yarn hints and tips
As with furry and fuzzy yarns, these yarns are best shown off with simple stitches – if you use any complicated or fancy stitches, they just won't be seen amid the fuzziness of the knitted fabric. If you are knitting an item that has a right side and a wrong side, and you want to get the strands and tufts on one side of the fabric to show them off in all their glory, simply pull them through with a crochet hook. These yarns can also be a little tricky to handle, as it can be hard to see each individual stitch on the needle. Again, work in a good light, and slow down if you tend to be a speedy knitter. On the positive side, however, these yarns are often quite substantial, so tend to be quick to knit up on larger-size needles.

Break out the bubbly: bouclé yarn

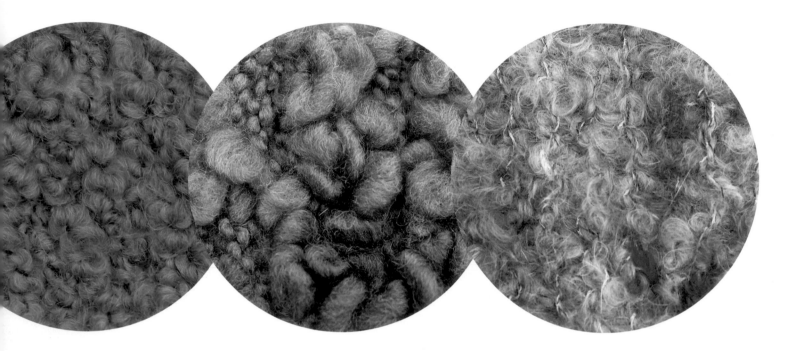

What is it?

Bouclé yarn has a core thread bunched up with another yarn with more bulk to give a very textural effect when knitted or crocheted, full of loops, curls, bubbles and bobbles. These yarns tend to be made from natural fibres such as wool and cotton. They are available in a variety of weights, from light-weight yarns with little loops, to chunky yarns with dense bobbles. These yarns are wonderfully tactile and extremely versatile.

What can I make with it?

I've used a luscious bouclé yarn for a large floor cushion, featuring a drop-stitch pattern that really shows off the unique texture of this yarn (pages 42–44). The friendly, bobbly faces of a children's kitty backpack and lion pyjama case (pages 50–55) are also made from bouclé. This yarn can be pretty robust, so is useful for children's items that may receive a lot of wear and tear. I also used a hybrid of bouclé and ribbon yarn to give a contemporary update to the sophisticated cloche hats of the flapper era; this yarn when knitted up produces a soft yet dense texture somewhat like towelling.

What's it for?

Bouclé yarn can knit up to quite a dense texture, so is ideal for accessories to protect you from the cold; try it for lush winter-weight scarves, or a curly-textured beanie hat.

Yarn hints and tips

Bouclé yarns can be a little difficult to work with, as the loops of the yarn can get snagged on the needle; it's important to keep the yarn taut as you work. You might find you have to knit more slowly than usual in order to avoid snarling up the yarn.

Bouclé yarn is distinguished by its curls and snarls; it is available in a range of weights from the light and loopy to a chunky yarn that is almost matted-looking.

Tie it with a ribbon: ribbon yarns

Ribbon yarns are a glamorous option – lustrous and fluid, and often shot through with sparkle.

What is it?
Knitting or crocheting with ribbon is quite special. The flat strands knit up beautifully to give a fabric that has a satiny sheen and a lovely soft feel. Ribbons are quite often created from synthetic fibres, although some combine synthetics with cotton and wool. These yarns vary in texture; some veer towards the wild with eyelash variations, while others are smooth and sinuous. My favourites are ones that are dyed in an interesting way to give the finished piece a multi-tonal dimension.

What can I make with it?
I have shown off the fluid texture of ribbon yarn in a wonderfully slinky scarf (pages 68–71). I have also used a ribbon yarn in a lustrous nylon-and-mohair-mix ribbon yarn teamed with spangly lurex for a glamorous hipster belt (pages 102–105).

What's it for?
Ribbon yarns often knit or crochet up into a fabric with a lovely drape, making them ideal for elegant shawls, draping dresses and silky throws. They are also perfect for making fringes, for example to edge a scarf or shawl.

Yarn hints and tips
Ribbon yarns are fairly easy to handle and tend to be quite chunky, so they work up satisfyingly quickly on larger-size needles. However, one problem you might find is that because the yarn is so sheeny and smooth, the stitches may drop off your needle and cause an accidental ladder in the knitted fabric. Using bamboo needles may help, as the bamboo grips on to the yarn more than slippery aluminium needles do. You might need to knit a little more slowly than usual, and keep a crochet hook handy to pick up any dropped stitches.

Chunky monkey: slubbed and super-chunky yarns

What is it?

It seems like only yesterday that medium-weight (aran) yarns were the chunkiest yarns you could buy. Now we have an explosion of super-bulky wools (and these yarns tend to be wool) all clamouring for our extra-large needles. Slubbed yarns are hybrids that vary in thickness from very, very skinny to super-chubby. I've put slubbed yarns in the same family as chunky, as they tend to work best when knitted on the same larger-sized needles.

What can I make with it?

I've used a slubbed wool yarn for a summery crocheted shrug (pages 72–75), and some gloriously colourful bulky wool for the ingenious pebble-shaped pillows (pages 30–33) and a cosy capelet for a child (pages 60–63).

What's it for?

These yarns are robust and resilient; a slubbed yarn would look fantastic as a cosy rug to add colour to a favourite room, while bulky-weight wool creates sturdy bags and wonderfully warm garments such as zip-up jackets and cosy winter hats.

Yarn hints and tips

Wool is generally an easy yarn to work with. With slubbed yarns, you might feel that your tension is very wobbly, as the yarn changes between thick and thin parts, but it will even out over all. Also, if you're used to thinner needles, the fat needles needed for this work may feel clumsy and awkward. Stick with it – you'll soon adapt – and take a break if you feel you are straining your wrists or shoulders.

Slubbed and chunky yarns have a wonderfully robust and woolly texture.

The best of the rest...

All taped up: tape yarns

Tape yarns are flat, woven yarns that look a little like cotton jersey or T-shirt material. They are available in both synthetic and natural fibres. The texture of these yarns is very flat and even.

In this book, I've used tape yarn for a slinkily glamorous camisole top (pages 76–79) and for a delightful dog jumper in a linen tape yarn (pages 94–97).

Tape yarns work best for garments, particularly body-skimming, drapey garments, such as crocheted shawls and well-fitted sweaters and vest tops.

These yarns are easy to handle and knit up quickly. One thing you might need to look out for is that these yarns can be fairly heavy, and the knitted or crocheted fabric can 'drop'. If you are making a garment and want to make sure it fits well without sagging, measure the work hanging off the needles, not when it's laid out flat.

Hot metal: lurex and metallic yarns

Lurex and metallic yarns have a crisp, hard texture and tend to come in bright, glinting, jewel-like colours. I wouldn't recommend them for making garments – they would be too harsh and scratchy worn directly against the skin – but their glitter and glitz are wonderful for fun accessories or to add a touch of sparkle when added to another yarn.

I've used lurex for some gloriously kitschy purses and make-up bags (pages 90–93), and for the spangly edgings on the crocheted belt (pages 102–105). Metallic threads also add glints and glimmer to the Bollywood bag (pages 106–108) and the Giddy gilet (pages 64–66).

Lurex yarns don't have the softest handle, so you might find it easier to knit them with smooth metal needles rather than the more 'grippy' bamboo needles.

Champagne and caviar: the luxury yarns

The two-ball projects in this book are an ideal excuse to splash out on some of the more luscious luxury yarns that are available. These are the yarns for really special items, made in the most sumptuous of natural fibres: cashmere, silk, alpaca or angora.

I've used pure alpaca to make a silkily soft heart-shaped bedwarmer (pages 26–29), while the Two-Tone Twist scarf (pages 80–83) features a truly heady mixture of extravagant yarns: silk, cashmere, angora, alpaca, kid mohair and camel.

Natural luxury fibres are wonderfully tactile and ideal for items worn next to the skin. Many budgets won't stretch to a whole garment made out of a luxury yarn, so keep things small and simple: scarves, hats, gloves and cushions are the best way to appreciate these beautiful fabrics.

Feather-weight fibres: mohair

Mohair is a lovely light-weight and airy yarn. The filaments of fuzzy yarn create a soft halo of colour floating above the surface of the main fabric.

I used mohair for the feather-soft baby slippers (pages 56–59). Mohair also adds a hazy touch to the lustrous ribbon yarn of the crocheted belt (pages 102–105).

Mohair can be a little itchy on its own; many yarns mix mohair with other yarns, including silk, to soften it a little. Mohair is not substantial or resilient enough for items that receive a lot of wear and tear, but comes into its own for light items such as shawls and scarves; cobwebby lace stitches look particularly beautiful when worked in mohair.

Mohair can be tricky to work with, because of its fine strands and the fuzziness of the yarn. Plastic or casein needles may be your best option to handle the yarn.

lost in translation

One thing you might need to be aware of is that knitting and crochet terms in the US and the UK are often different. The most confusion arises when the same term is used to refer to completely different things (this is a particular headache in crochet). In this book, I've favoured US terms and put the UK equivalent in brackets. Just so you have a handy reference, we've gathered all the potentially troublesome or confusing terms in one place here. This will also be helpful if you are fluent in one crafting language but are using a pattern from another part of the world.

Weighty issues

It's important to know the weight of yarn, particularly when you are looking for a substitute. Here are the common terms:

US yarn weights	UK yarn weights
Super fine weight	2ply
Fine weight	4ply
Light weight	DK
Medium weight	aran
Bulky weight	chunky
Super bulky weight	super chunky

Needles in a haystack

Whereas knitters in most parts of the world buy needles that are sized on the metric system, the US uses its own idiosyncratic needle sizes.

US knitting needle sizes	UK knitting needle sizes
0	2mm
1	2.25mm
	2.5mm
2	2.75mm
	3mm
3	3.25mm
4	3.5mm
5	3.75mm
6	4mm
7	4.5mm
8	5mm
9	5.5mm
10	6mm
10½	6.5mm
	7mm
	7.5mm
11	8mm
13	9mm
15	10mm
16	12mm
17	12.75mm
19	15mm

Getting your hooks in

The same applies to crochet hook sizes; international crocheters use the metric system, whereas the US has its own unique system.

US crochet hook sizes	UK crochet hook sizes
B1	2.5mm
C2	2.75mm
D3	3.25mm
E4	3.5mm
F5	3.75mm
G6	4mm
7	4.5mm
H8	5mm
I9	5.5mm
J10	6mm
K10½	6.5mm
L11	8mm
M/N13	9mm
N/P15	10mm
P/Q	15mm

The knitty gritty

Some terms in knitting are different for the US and the UK:

US knitting term	UK knitting term
bind off	cast off
gauge	tension
stockinette stitch	stocking stitch
reverse stockinette stitch	reverse stocking stitch
seed stitch	moss stitch

Hooking up

Some terms in crochet are different for the US and the UK: in addition, the same term can be used to refer to different stitches. Make sure you know which terms your pattern is using or you could end up with some very peculiar results! In this book, I use US terms.

US crochet term	UK crochet term
slip stitch	single crochet
single crochet	double crochet
half-double crochet	half treble
double crochet	treble
treble crochet	double treble
double treble crochet	treble treble

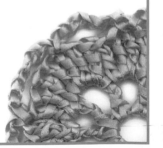

The long and the short of it

To save space and cut down repetition, knitting and crochet patterns often use abbreviations. These lists are not comprehensive guides to every possible abbreviation, but do comprise the terms used for the projects in this book.

Knitting abbreviations

Dec 1	decrease by 1 stitch, generally by knitting or purling 2 stitches together
Inc 1	increase by 1 stitch, either by picking up the loop of the next stitch on the row before and placing it on the left-hand needle, or working a new stitch between the two current ones
K	knit
K2tog	knit 2 stitches together (decrease by 1 stitch)
K3tog	knit 3 stitches together (decrease by 2 stitches)
K2togtbl	knit 2 stitches together through the back loop (decrease by 1 stitch)
K3togtbl	knit 3 stitches together through the back loop (decrease by 2 stitches)
M1	make 1 stitch (increase by 1 stitch), either by picking up the loop of the next stitch on the row before and placing it on the left-hand needle, or working a new stitch between the two current ones
M1k	make 1 knit stitch (increase by 1 stitch)
M1p	make 1 purl stitch (increase by 1 stitch)
P	purl
P2tog	purl 2 stitches together (decrease by 1 stitch)
P3tog	purl 3 stitches together (decrease by 2 stitches)
P2togtbl	purl 2 stitches together through the back loop (decrease by 1 stitch)
P3togtbl	purl 3 stitches together through the back loop (decrease by 2 stitches)
Patt	pattern (i.e. knit in the established pattern)
Patt2tog	pattern 2 stitches together; you will knit or purl two stitches together depending on the run of the pattern (decrease by 1 stitch)
Psso	pass slipped stitch over (decrease by 1 stitch)
Rem	remaining
RS	right side
Ss	slip 1 stitch from the left-hand needle to the right-hand needle
St(s)	stitch(es)
St st	stockinette stitch; knit 1 row, purl 1 row
WS	wrong side
Yo	yarnover

Crochet abbreviations (US)

ch	chain
dc	double crochet
dtr	double treble
hdc	half double crochet
tr	treble
sc	single crochet
ss	slip stitch
st	stitch

Note: See Hooking up, left, for UK equivalent terms

essential knitting techniques

I presume that most people picking up this book will already be knitters or crocheters who are looking to try something new, rather than complete novices. If in fact you don't know a knitting needle from a trussing needle, don't worry: all the patterns in this book are pretty straightforward. If there is something you don't know, or your technique is rusty, all the knitting and crochet techniques needed to complete the projects are set out in the next few pages.

Squaring up: the importance of gauge

For most projects you will need to knit (or crochet) a gauge square (also known as a gauge swatch). Each pattern includes gauge instructions that state how many stitches and how many rows there should be to a 4in (10cm) square in a given stitch and using a given size of needles or hook. For example, the Colourful capelet (pages 60–63) states that you should achieve a gauge of 10 sts and 15 rows to 4in (10cm) square over stockinette stitch using size 11 (8mm) needles. You should aim to achieve the same measurements. This is important because if your gauge is off, your finished item will come out a different size from the one required. This isn't crucial for items such as scarves, but is important for garments that need to fit well.

If your tension is tight and the gauge square comes out too small, try again with larger needles or hook. If your tension is loose and the gauge square comes out too large, try again with smaller needles or hook.

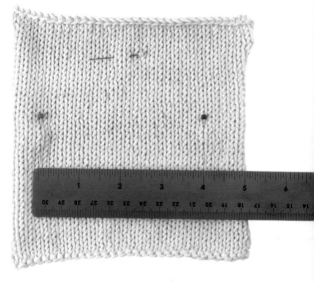

When measuring the gauge swatch, mark your stitches with some pins with coloured heads to give you a clear place to measure from.

Casting on

There are many, many methods of casting on, but this is a quick and simple one that creates a firm, neat edge.

Holding one needle in your right hand, make a loop of yarn with your left hand, as shown in the diagram left. Turn the loop inwards (i.e. from left to right) to place it on the needle. Pull the yarn taut. Repeat until you have the required number of stitches.

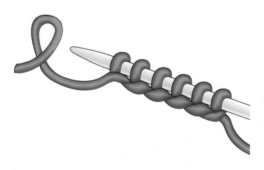

Binding off

Knit your first stitch as normal (see page 17). Then knit your second stitch. When you have two loops on your right-hand needle, insert your left-hand needle into the first loop (1), pass it over the second loop (2), and drop the stitch off the needle. This is your first bound-off stitch. Now knit the next stitch, and, again, pass the first stitch on your right-hand needle over the second stitch and drop it off the needle. Repeat until all stitches have been bound off.

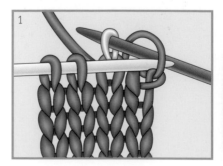

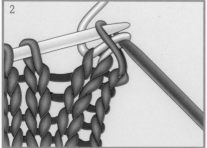

Knit stitch

Insert your right-hand needle from front to back into the first loop on your left-hand needle (1). Wrap your yarn around the tip of the right-hand needle, from back to front (2). Slide the tip of the right-hand needle down to pick up this new loop of yarn (3), and slip the loop off the left-hand needle. This is the first stitch. If you knit every row, you make garter stitch.

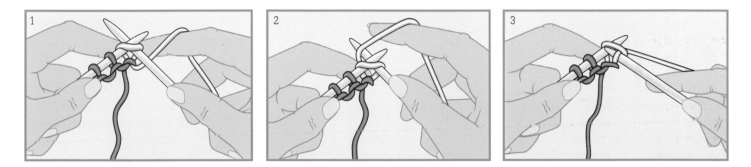

Purl stitch

Insert your right-hand needle into the first loop on your left-hand needle, inserting the needle from right to left through the front of the loop (1). Wrap your yarn around the tip of the right-hand needle, counterclockwise (2). Slide the tip of the right-hand needle back to pick up this loop of new yarn (3), and slide the loop off the left-hand needle. This is the first stitch. Once you know both knit and purl stitches, you can make garter stitch, stockinette stitch, seed stitch and ribbing in all its variations.

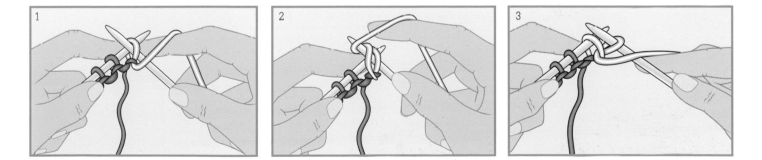

Increasing stitches

There are a number of ways to increase stitches; here are two simple methods.

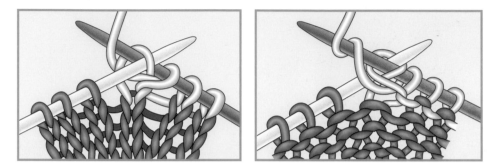

Inc 1

Work into the front of the stitch on the left-hand needle as usual, but instead of slipping the stitch onto the right-hand needle, work into the back of the stitch. Then slip the stitch onto the right-hand needle. You can use this increase on both knit and purl rows.

tip When yarnovers are used to create buttonholes they are usually teamed with a k2tog to keep the overall number of stitches in the row correct. Remember to work the k2tog or your stitch count will be thrown out. Yarnovers are also used decoratively; the holes in intricate lace patterns are usually created by this method.

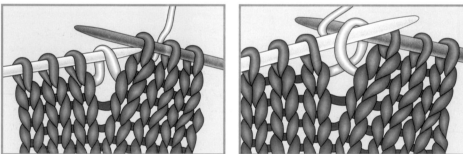

Make 1 (M1)

At the point where you need to make the increase, insert the tip of your left-hand needle into the horizontal strand of yarn between the two stitches you are working on. Lift this strand onto the left-hand needle. Now knit into the back of this loop and slip it on to the right-hand needle.

Yarnover (Yo)

This is a method of increasing stitches that leaves a 'hole' in the fabric. This is the method I have used to create the buttonholes for the bedwarmer (pages 26–29) and the baby slippers (pages 56–59). At the point where you need to make the increase, simply wrap the yarn, from front to back, round your right-hand needle to form an extra loop there. Then knit your next stitch as usual. On the return row, you knit this strand as if it were a normal stitch, but it will leave a hole in the fabric.

Decreasing stitches

There are a number of ways to decrease stitches, according to whether you are on a knit or a purl row.

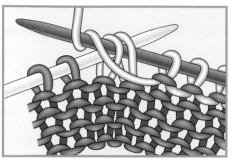

Knit two stitches together (K2tog)

Insert your right-hand needle from front to back through both the second and the first stitches on your left-hand needle, and knit them together as if they were one stitch.

Purl two stitches together (P2tog)

Insert your right-hand needle from right to left through the front of the first two stitches on your left-hand needle, and purl them together as if they were one stitch.

K3tog and P3 tog

Follow the instructions as set out left, but insert your needle through three stitches rather than two and knit or purl these three together as one stitch.

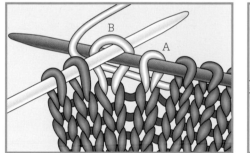

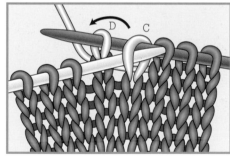

Slip one, knit one, pass slipped stitch over

This decreasing method is used for the Super-soft slippers (pages 56–59); passing the slipped stitch over is known by the abbreviation psso.

Insert your right-hand needle into the first stitch on your left-hand needle as if you were going to knit it, but simply slip it on to the right-hand needle (A). Knit the next stitch (B). Insert your left-hand needle into the loop of the slipped stitch on the right-hand needle (it will be the second loop – C), and pass it over the first stitch (D; this is the same action as if you were binding off the stitch).

tip When decreasing at the edge of the work on a piece where the edges will be visible (the front panels of the gilet, for example – see pages 64–67), it's a good idea to work the decrease one or two stitches from the end of the row. This creates a nicely rounded shape, rather than the more jagged one produced if the decrease is worked right at the end of the row.

Special techniques

Some of the projects feature more advanced techniques, which we explain below.

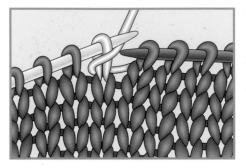

Short rows

Short rows are a way of shaping knitting. This technique involves knitting part-way along a row and then turning the work to knit along the other side. This extra knitting creates a curved shape. I've used this method for shaping the Pucker-up purses (pages 90–93).

Knit to the point where you need to turn the work. Slip the next stitch from the left-hand needle to the right-hand needle. Bring the yarn from the back of the work so it lies at the front of the work. Then slip the slipped stitch from the right-hand needle back on to the left-hand needle, and bring the yarn from the front to the back of the work. You have 'wrapped' the turning stitch, which means that the extra rows won't leave a distinct gap or hole in the knitted fabric. Now you can turn the work and purl back across the row.

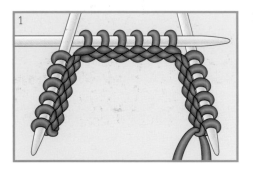

Knitting with double-pointed needles

Knitting with a set of four double-pointed needles rather than two straight needles means that you can knit a tube shape in one piece, without seams. This is ideal for socks, sleeves, and as we've used them, armwarmers (pages 98–101). The work is spread out onto three of the needles, arranged in a triangle shape, and the fourth needle is used as the working needle. You cast your stitches on to one needle, and then divide them evenly between the three needles (1).

Bring the needles together to form a triangle, and you are ready to knit your first stitch, using the fourth needle (2). Make sure you pull the yarn up tightly once you have knitted the first stitch; it is quite common for there to be a gap at this point that may become quite noticeable (it will look like a ladder) after a few rounds.

Make sure all the cast-on stitches are facing inwards as you knit the first round; don't let them become twisted. Once you have knitted all the stitches off the first needle on to the working needle, the first needle will be free, and now becomes your working needle.

This method of working will probably feel quite awkward, at least for the first few rounds, as you grapple with all the needles. It may help to rest the knitting on a tabletop or other flat surface until you get past this point.

tip If you know that your tension tends to be quite loose, you might find bamboo the best option when working with double-pointed needles. Bamboo will hold on to the yarn more than metal or plastic, so should stop your stitches slipping off the ends of the needles and make the process of knitting in the round more stable.

Three-needle bind-off

We use a three-needle bind-off for the Colourful capelet (pages 60–63) and the Sassy stripe armwarmers (pages 98–101). This is a neat bind-off that joins the seams together (so there's no need to sew them together – a bonus for all of us who prefer knitting to sewing!).

Hold your two working needles together in your left hand, tips pointing to the right, with the right sides of the work inwards and the wrong sides outwards. Take a third needle of the same size in your right hand and insert it through the first stitch on each left-hand needle. Knit the stitches together. Repeat for the second two stitches. When you have two loops on your right-hand needle, bind them off as usual (see page 16) by passing the first loop over the second and dropping it off the needle. Repeat for all the stitches on the left-hand needle.

When you hold the right sides together to bind off, as in the diagram shown right, the seam will be on the wrong side. Note, however, that for the Colourful capelet, you hold the wrong sides (the purl sides) together to bind off so that the seam forms a ridge that shows on the right side – it is a decorative seam that is meant to show.

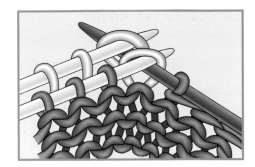

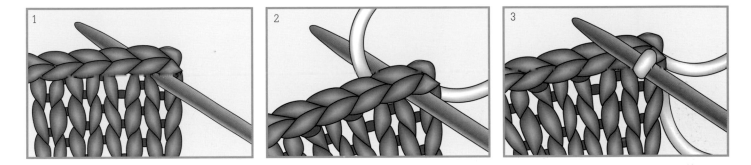

Picking up stitches

You pick up stitches from a bound-off or finished edge to turn them into live stitches to add some more work to the piece. This is a common way, for example, of adding a collar to a sweater. We pick up stitches in the Colourful capelet (pages 60–63) to form the hood.

You need only one needle to pick up stitches. Hold the fabric, right side towards you, in your left hand, and insert the needle held in your right hand through the first stitch you need to pick up (1). Wrap the yarn around the needle (2) and pull the yarn through the fabric back to the front of the work (3). This is your first picked-up stitch. Repeat until you have picked up all the stitches you need according to your pattern instructions.

tip When you finish a knitted or crocheted piece, take the time to block it. This process shapes up your work to even out any wonkiness or to set the piece into a particular shape – a square with crisp straight edges and right angles, for example, or a properly rounded curved edge.

You will need a slightly padded surface. It's possible to buy special blocking boards, but you can improvise a suitable surface with a board wrapped in a couple of fluffy towels. An ironing board will also work well. Pin your piece out on to the board, shaping it into the size and shape you want it to be. Then cover it with a damp cloth and press it using a hot iron. Leave the piece to dry completely.

essential crochet techniques

If you have never tried crochet before, here's your opportunity. The crochet projects in this book are simple but satisfying; the basic techniques are set out below, and you'll soon be itching to have a go. Hold the work firmly with the first finger and thumb of your left hand, and use your right hand to control the hook. Hold the hook like a pencil; it should rest in your hand comfortably. When you are trying out the techniques for the first time, don't use a fuzzy yarn, as it is difficult to see the stitches.

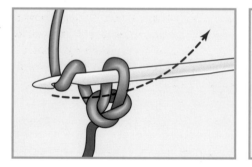

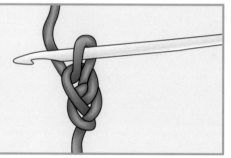

Chain (ch)

To start any piece of crochet, you need first to crochet a chain as your foundation row.

Tie a slipknot in the end of your yarn and place the loop on your hook. Wrap the yarn clockwise over the hook, and pull the yarn through the loop on the hook to form a fresh loop. This is one chain; repeat for as many chain stitches as the pattern instructions state.

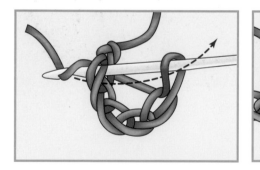

tip Don't forget that I'm using US crochet terms throughout, see p. 15 Hooking up, for UK equivalents.

Joining a chain into a circle

Crochet patterns are often worked in circular motifs (see the Fruit fizz coasters, pages 38–41, and the crocheted belt, pages 102–105). When you have worked your chain, you need to join it into a circle.

Insert your hook into the first chain, wrap the yarn around the hook, and pull the yarn through both the first chain and the loop of the last chain of the row (that is, the loop already on the hook).

Slip stitch (ss)

Slip stitch is a stitch that has no height, but is very useful for joining crochet pieces together (this is how the roundels of the crochet belt are joined together; see pages 102–105).

Insert the hook under the top two strands of the stitch beneath (these stitches will look like a 'V' shape). Wrap the yarn over the hook, and pull the yarn through the work and through the loop on the hook.

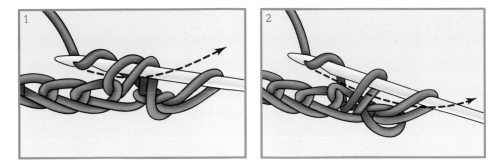

Single crochet (sc)

This is the basic crochet stitch; all the other stitches described here are simply taller versions of this stitch.

Insert the hook under the top two strands of the stitch beneath. Wrap the yarn over the hook and pull the yarn through (1). Wrap the yarn over the hook again and pull it through both the loops on the hook (2). This is one stitch.

Half double crochet (hdc)

Half double crochet is the next tallest stitch. Wrap the yarn over the hook and then insert it under the top two strands of the stitch beneath. Wrap the yarn over again, and pull it through the work (1). You will have three loops on the hook. Wrap the yarn over again and pull it through all three loops on the hook (2). This is one stitch.

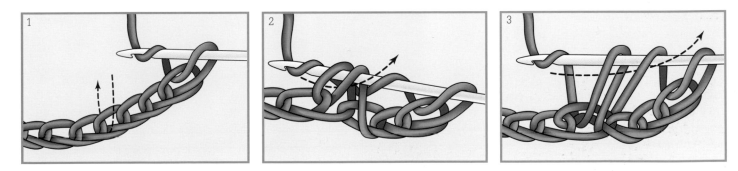

Double crochet

This is the next tallest stitch.

Wrap the yarn over the hook and then insert it under the top two strands of the stitch beneath (1). Wrap the yarn over, and pull it through the work (2). You have three loops on the hook. Wrap the yarn over again and pull it through the first two loops on the hook (3). Wrap the yarn over again, and pull it through the two remaining loops on the hook. This is one stitch.

Treble crochet (tr)

Treble crochet is created in exactly the same way, but is simply one stitch taller. You start off by wrapping the yarn over *twice* before pulling it through the work, then continue as normal.

Double treble (dtr)

You're probably starting to see a pattern here…Double treble is the next tallest stitch. Start off by wrapping the yarn over *three times* before pulling it through the work, then continue as before.

delicious details

If you have invested a lot of time and effort knitting or crocheting a project, it makes sense to take care over the finishing details too. I think a gourmet yarn deserves to be teamed with special trimmings such as pretty beads, special buttons, toning ribbons, tassels and pom poms. Buttons and other decorative details can make or break a garment, and it is worth spending a little time searching out the perfect trimming. Your local craft and yarn stores are the best first point of call, but consider other sources such as Internet boutiques and eBay.

Pom poms

I think pom poms are a great way to trim handmade pieces. You can buy ready-made ones, and you can also buy pom pom-making kits, but it's simple enough to make your own.

Get two pieces of circular cardboard with a central hole cut out of the middle (i.e., something that looks like a flat doughnut). Hold the pieces together and wrap your yarn around the ring of the 'doughnut', until the whole ring is covered. Cut through the loops of yarn on the outside of the ring (pull the two pieces of cardboard apart and cut the yarn between them). Then take a length of yarn and tie it firmly between the two cardboard pieces. Fasten with a secure knot. Cut out the cardboard pieces, and fluff up the pom pom so it's a nice round shape.

Beads are a lovely addition to a handmade item. They can transform a quite plain, mundane piece into something that looks like jewellery.

Pom poms make a great finishing touch to a handmade piece, whether made from the same yarn or in some contrast yarn.

Buttons don't just have to be used as a humble cardigan fastening; they can be sewn on to accessories purely as decoration.

home

Artisan yarns and knitted and crocheted items for the home
make perfect partners. A cushion created in a bright bouclé yarn,
for example, will add both a lively accent colour and intriguing
texture to an interior.

But creating for the home isn't all about cushions – hand-knitted
and crocheted cushions are top of my list, I admit, but there are a
number of items that are simple to make and that really show off
the properties of a gourmet yarn.

In this section, we have projects for all the most important rooms
in a home. For the conservatory or to use on a garden bench, we
have pebble-shaped cushions knitted in wools with an unusual
sprayed and splattered effect. For the kitchen and dining room,
we have jar covers and coasters that take a fun, contemporary
twist on traditional crocheted doilies and show off the fresh, crisp
colours of mercerized cottons and satin ribbons. For the bedroom,
we have a lusciously soft alpaca bedwarmer, while for the lounge
we have a bumper-sized bouclé floor cushion. Finally, for every
crafter's favourite workspot, wherever in the home it may be, we
have a unique raggy-ribbon denim-lined storage cube – perfect
to hold all your knitting and crochet notions in one place.

warm-hearted
bedwarmer

This small, sumptuously soft heart-shaped cushion is just the thing to snuggle into when you feel the cold.

When driving through farmland in most countries, cows are two-a-penny, sheep are pretty commonplace, and pigs more rare, but still not stop-the-car-what-was-that rare. However, when you first see a llama or an alpaca grazing in a meadow, that's worth slamming on the brakes for. After spotting a herd (or is it a pride? or a school?) of llamas in a field one day, I headed straight to the luxury section of my local yarn store in the hope of finding a few hanks of llama wool. I found the next best thing – pure alpaca. Apparently, alpacas make delightful companions, which is why many artisan yarn producers are adding alpacas to their flocks and producing delicious new gourmet yarns.

I decided to use alpaca for this piece because of its warmth and beautiful softness. As an alternative to alpaca, a soft, lush, wool yarn will also work well (see page 29). To transform the cushion into a bedwarmer, you can fill it with a cherry-stone bag and lavender sachets. The cherry-stone pad can be heated in the oven; it keeps its heat longer than a traditional hot-water bottle. (It can also be used as a cold compress if chilled in the freezer.) The heat of the cherry stones releases the soothing and relaxing aroma of the lavender.

The alpaca's luxurious fibre makes wonderfully soft and warm items.

what you need and what you need to know...

yarn
2 x 1¾oz (50g) balls super-bulky-weight (super-chunky)
   alpaca or pure new wool

needles
1 pair size 15 (10mm) needles

notions
Stitch holder
Darning needle
Polyester or cotton wadding
Sewing thread
10in x 16in (25cm x 40cm) of cotton fabric in
   a toning colour
2 large buttons about 1¼in (3cm) across
Small lavender bag and small bag of cherry stones

size
Different yarns will knit up different sized bedwarmers.
   A super-chunky yarn will knit up one about 10in
   (25cm) across, while a more refined bulky yarn will
   produce an item around 8in (20cm) across.

gauge
Maintaining gauge is not essential for this project;
   just keep your stitches even and you should be fine.

pattern note The heart is knitted up in
three pieces. The front heart-shaped piece is knitted in
stockinette stitch with a band of seed stitch across the
middle. The back is knitted in two pieces, top and bottom,
which are fastened together with two buttons. Yarnovers
(yo) are used to create the buttonholes.

Alpaca fibre can be spun finely to give a cashmere-soft yarn, or left as thicker, unspun, strands to give a more fleecy effect – the type I used for this project.

pattern

Back (bottom piece)
Cast on 3 sts.
Row 1 Purl.
Row 2 (RS) Inc 1, knit to end, inc 1. 5 sts.
Cont in st st, increasing 2 sts as set every
RS row until 25 sts.
Row 23 (WS) (k1, p1) to last stitch,
k1. 25 sts.
Rep last row to set up seed stitch
pattern.
Row 25 (k1, p1) 3 times, k2tog,
(k1, p1) 4 times, k1, k2tog (p1, k1) 3 times.
23 sts.
Row 26 (Buttonhole row) (k1, p1)
3 times, k1, yo, (k1, p1) 4 times, k1, yo,
(k1, p1) 3 times, k1. 25 sts.
Work 1 row, then bind off keeping seed
stitch pattern intact.

Back (top piece)
Cast on 25 sts and work 2 rows in st st,
beginning with a knit row.
Row 3 K2togtbl, knit to last 2 sts,
k2tog. 23 sts.
Row 4 Purl.
Row 5 K2togtbl, knit to last 2 sts,
k2tog. 21 sts.
Row 6 P9, p2tog, p10. 20 sts.
Row 7 K2togtbl, k8, turn and work
on these 9 sts only, putting remaining
stitches on a stitch holder.
Row 8 P2tog, p7. 8 sts.
Row 9 K2togtbl, k4, k2tog. 6 sts.
Row 10 P2tog, p4. 5 sts.
Row 11 K2togtbl, k3. 4 sts.
Row 12 Bind off remaining 4 sts.

With RS facing, rejoin yarn to the work
and remaining 10 sts.
Row 1 K8, k2tog. 9 sts.
Row 2 P7, p2tog. 8 sts.
Row 3 K2togtbl, k4, k2tog. 6 sts.
Row 4 P4, p2tog. 5 sts.
Row 5 K3, k2tog. 4 sts.
Row 6 Bind off remaining 4 sts.

Front
Cast on 3 sts.
Row 1 Purl.
Row 2 (RS) Inc 1, k3, inc 1. 5 sts.
Row 3 Purl.
Cont in st st, increasing by 2 sts as set
every RS row until 25 sts.
Row 23 (WS) (k1, p1) to last stitch, k1.
Work 4 further rows in seed stitch
pattern.
Row 28 K2togtbl, knit to end, k2tog.
23 sts.
Row 29 Purl.
Row 30 K2togtbl, knit to end, k2tog.
21 sts.
Row 31 P9, p2tog, p10. 20 sts.
Row 32 K2togtbl, k8, turn and work
on these 9 sts only, putting remaining
stitches on a stitch holder.
Row 33 P2tog, p7. 8 sts.
Row 34 K2togtbl, k4, k2tog. 6 sts.
Row 35 P2tog, p4. 5 sts.
Row 36 K2togtbl, k3. 4 sts.
Row 37 Bind off remaining 4 sts.

With RS facing, rejoin yarn to the work
and remaining 10 sts.
Row 1 K8, k2tog. 9 sts.
Row 2 P7, p2tog. 8 sts.
Row 3 K2togtbl, k4, k2tog. 6 sts.
Row 4 P4, p2tog. 5 sts.
Row 5 K3, k2tog. 4 sts.
Row 6 Bind off remaining 4 sts.

tip You can buy cherry stones ready washed and ready for use, or simply keep all the stones from your family's next bowl of cherries. Make sure the stones are very clean and dry before using. To warm up the cherry-stone bag, heat it in an oven at a maximum 150 degrees or in a microwave oven up to 600W for two minutes. To use as a cold compress, chill the bag in a freezer for an hour.

Take some care over what buttons you use; they should be an appropriate size and tone in attractively with the colour of yarn you have chosen.

making up

Darn in any loose ends. Pin out the knitting, right-side down, on to a padded surface or blocking board to form the correct heart shape. Cover with a damp cloth and press the wrong side gently with a hot iron. Leave to dry completely. Lay the front heart piece right-side down. Lay the top heart piece of the back on top, then position the bottom heart piece on top, with an overlay where the pieces meet. Mark where the buttonholes are, then sew on the buttons. Now sew the front to the back, sewing in the overlap of the button band.

Take the lining cotton and cut a piece as long as the opening on the back of the heart, and 10in (25cm) deep. Fold ⅜in (1cm) over on each of the long ends and slipstitch ends into place. With right side in, fold the fabric in with hemmed edges, leaving a 1¼in (3cm) gap in the middle. Now stitch across the corners and snip off any excess fabric. Stitch the short ends into place, creating a long, thin envelope shape. Stuff the heart with soft padding and slip the cotton envelope into place. Take the piece of cotton and slipstitch it into place, ensuring the cotton envelope does not obstruct the buttonholes. You may need to slipstitch the edges of the button flap together to hide any untidiness at the sides. Place a cherry-stone pad and a lavender bag into the pocket and button up.

tip You can vary the amount of padding or stuffing depending on whether you want a relatively squashy bedwarmer or a firmer, more resilient one. There are a number of materials available to use for the filling, from polystyrene balls like those used to fill bean bags, to more spongy, fibrous wadding.

This pattern can be used to make a pretty and simple heart cushion. Make two front pieces and stitch together the padding as you go.

pebble
pillows

These cushions are like little rocks that are soft to the touch and add some tongue-in-cheek humour to a room or a garden bench.

One of the most innovative ways in which yarns are being updated for the modern knitting age is by the addition of surface pattern. Wools and cottons are being overprinted with patterns, variations on colours and spray-painted by hand to create unique yarns.

Spray-painted yarns are available as bulky-weight (chunky) yarns, as used here, and also as fine, gauzy yarns that have a lovely ethereal look. The colour effect ranges from those that look as though the colour was applied with a fairy's wing, and those that look as if they've had a fight in a very messy paint shop. So, graffiti or goddess, it's your choice.

With these pillows, the spray-paint effect really comes into its own when the yarn is knitted up, creating a piece of fabric that is mottled and spattered. To my eye, this effect has the hard-and-soft qualities of pebbles and stones, which inspired their use for these pillows. The colour combinations used are natural and neutral (although they could never be called bland and boring), so will fit into any colour scheme.

This yarn has been painted, sprayed and splattered to give an organic appeal.

what you need and what you need to know...

yarn
2 x 3½oz (100g) balls of spray-painted bulky-weight (chunky) wool in natural shades

needles
1 pair size 15 (10mm) needles

notions
Stitch holders

Darning needle

Polyester beads or soft polyester stuffing to fill

size
Small pebble is about 14½ by 12½in (37 by 32cm)

Large pebble is about 18½ by 17½in (47 by 45cm)

gauge
9 sts and 11 rows to 4in (10cm) square over stockinette stitch using size 15 (10mm) needles

pattern note Each pebble is constructed from three pieces: the front, the back, and a gusset to give depth to the pillow. The pebbly shape is created by increasing and decreasing stitches. Various decreases are used, including k2tog, p2tog, and k3tog (see page 19 for more on these techniques).

The spray-painted effect of this yarn creates unique colour combinations that are wonderfully organic-looking.

pattern

Small pebble: front
Cast on 12 sts.

Row 1 (RS) Inc 1, k12, inc 1. 14 sts.

Working in st st (next row purl), increase 1 st at each end of next 3 rows. 20 sts.

Row 5 K20, inc 1. 21 sts.

Row 6 Inc 1, purl to end. 22 sts.

Work 3 rows st st even (i.e., with no shaping).

Row 10 P2tog, p20, inc 1. 22 sts.

Work 2 rows st st even.

Row 13 Inc 1, k22. 23 sts.

Row 14 Purl.

Row 15 K20, k3tog. 21 sts.

Row 16 P21, inc 1. 22 sts.

Row 17 K19, k3tog. 20 sts.

Row 18 Purl.

Row 19 Inc 1, k20. 21 sts.

Row 20 Purl.

Row 21 Inc 1, k21. 22 sts.

Row 22 P2tog, p20. 21 sts.

Row 23 Inc 1, k19, k2tog. 21 sts.

Row 24 Purl.

Row 25 Inc 1, k19, k2tog. 21 sts.

Row 26 Purl.

Row 27 K2tog, k19. 20 sts.

Row 28 Purl.

Row 29 Inc 1, k20, inc 1. 22 sts.

Row 30 Purl.

Row 31 Cast on 3 sts, k25 (1st 3 k sts are over cast-on sts), inc 1. 26 sts.

Row 32 P24, p2tog. 25 sts.

Row 33 Cast on 3 sts, knit to end. 28 sts.

Row 34 P3tog, p22, p3tog. 24 sts.

Row 35 K2tog, k20, k2tog. 22 sts.

Row 36 Bind off loosely in purl.

Make back to match, reversing all shaping.

Small pebble: gusset
Cast on 4 sts.

Work 26 rows in st st, beginning with a knit row.

Row 27 Inc 1 at each end of row. 6 sts.

Work further 22 rows in st st even.

Row 50 Inc 1 at each end of next row. 8 sts.

Work further 17 rows in st st even.

Row 68 Dec 1 each end of next row. 6 sts.

Work further 26 rows in st st even.

Row 95 Dec 1 each end of next row. 4 sts.

Work 7 rows in st st even.

Row 103 Dec 1 st at beg next row. 3 sts.

Work further 20 rows in st st, and leave the stitches on a stitch holder.

Large pebble: front
Cast on 18 sts.

Row 1 (RS) Inc 1, k18, inc 1. 20 sts.

Row 2 Inc 1, p20, inc 1. 22 sts.

Row 3 Inc 1, k22. 23 sts.

Row 4 P23, inc 1. 24 sts.

Row 5 Inc 1, k24, inc 1. 26 sts.

Row 6 Purl.

Row 7 Cast on 3 sts, knit to end. 29 sts.

Work 2 rows st st even.

Row 10 Inc 1, p29, inc 1. 31 sts.

Work 2 rows st st even.

Row 13 Cast on 3 sts, k to end. 34 sts.

Row 14 Purl.

Row 15 K31, k3tog. 32 sts.

Row 16 P2tog, p30. 31 sts.

Row 17 Inc 1, k29, K2tog. 31 sts.

Row 18 Purl.

Row 19 Cast on 3 sts, k to last 2 sts, k2tog. 33 sts.

Row 20 Purl.

Row 21 K31, k2tog. 32 sts.

Row 22 P2tog, p30. 31 sts.

Row 23 K29, k2tog. 30 sts.

Row 24 P2tog, p28. 29 sts.
Row 25 K2tog, k25, k2tog. 27 sts.
Row 26 Purl.
Row 27 K2tog, k25. 26 sts.
Row 28 P24, p2tog. 25 sts.
Row 29 K2tog, k23. 24 sts.
Row 30 Inc 1, p24, inc 1. 26 sts.
Row 31 K26, inc 1. 27 sts.
Row 32 Inc 1, p27. 28 sts.
Row 33 K2tog, k26, inc 1. 28 sts.
Row 34 Inc 1, p26, p2tog. 28 sts.
Row 35 K2tog, k26, inc 1. 28 sts.
Row 36 Inc 1, p26, p2tog. 28 sts.
Row 37 K2tog, k26, inc 1. 28 sts.
Row 38 P26, p2tog. 27 sts.
Row 39 K2tog, k25. 26 sts.
Row 40 P24, p2tog. 25 sts.
Row 41 K2tog, k23. 24 sts.
Row 42 P22, p2tog. 23 sts.
Row 43 K2tog, k19, k2tog. 21 sts.
Row 44 P2tog, p17, p2tog. 19 sts.
Row 45 Knit.
Row 46 P2tog, p15, p2tog. 17 sts.
Row 47 K3tog, k11, k3tog. 13 sts.

Row 48 P2tog, p9, p2tog. 11 sts.
Bind off loosely.
Make back to match, reversing all shaping.

Large pebble: gusset
Cast on 6 sts.
Work 32 rows in st st, beginning with a knit row.
Row 33 Inc 1 at each end of next row. 8 sts.
Work further 22 rows in st st even.
Row 56 Inc 1 at each end of row. 10 sts.
Work further 17 rows in st st even.
Row 74 Dec 1 each end of row. 8 sts.
Work further 22 rows in st st even.
Row 97 Dec 1 each end of row. 6 sts.
Work 5 rows in st st even.
Row 103 Dec 1 st at beg row. 5 sts.
Work further 47 rows in st st even.
Row 151 Inc 1 at beg of row (6 sts) and keep all stitches on a stitch holder for making up.

tip The larger pebble is a slightly misshapen heart shape. To create your own misshapen pebble shape, simply add a few random increases or decreases into the pattern, marking clearly so you will know when to copy the shaping for the other side. If you decide to do this, buy an extra ball of yarn, just in case.

making up

Darn in any loose ends. Cover the pieces with a damp cloth and press on the wrong side (the purl side) with a hot iron. Pin the gusset to the side pieces, with the end join at the side for the small pebble and the side indent in the large pebble. Fill the pebble with polyester balls to make it firm but squishy, or with polyester stuffing for a softer rock. Sew the remaining side seams. If the gusset is too long, unravel a couple of rows until it has a good fit. If it is too short, knit a few more rows. Using a darning needle, join the stitches to the cast-on end using the needle to 'knit' the pieces together.

tip I always gravitate to pebbles on the beach that are shaped like hearts or familiar shapes, so this project was my homage to my cache of found stones. It's a lovely idea to take inspiration for knitting projects from nature or other found objects. Start a collection of beautiful things that appeal to you and see whether it inspires you to design your own unique items.

rainbow rags
storage cube

A riotous raggy-ribbon yarn teamed with well-worn denim fabric make up a colourful and robust storage cube.

There is a type of yarn that I like to call 'raggy ribbon'. It's part of the wild family, and it combines ribbon with tufts of ragged, torn fabrics. When I saw the raggy-ribbon yarn used here in the yarn store, I immediately thought of soft, worn denim jeans with frayed knees and ripped seams. Not because of the colour, which is quite a rainbow, but because of the fraying fronds that are wrapped in bright, silky thread.

My first inspiration was to use the yarn to knit an exuberantly colourful scarf to wear with a denim jacket. I then decided to match the yarn with an old pair of jeans to make a useful storage cube to keep all my knitting and crochet notions and yarns together. You can either sew the knitting to the denim lining and leave the cube quite squishy, or do as I have here and use pieces of stiff card to strengthen the sides and base to make the box more rigid and resilient. The jeans have lots of pockets in which you could keep smaller crafty equipment such as crochet hooks and buttons. This project is a great way to recycle old clothes – and a marvellous excuse to go out and buy a new pair of jeans!

This yarn is like old rag rugs with clumps of soft cotton and delicate, frayed edges.

what you need and what you need to know...

yarn
2 x 1¾oz (50g) balls of bulky-weight (chunky) raggy-ribbon yarn

needles
1 pair size 9 (5.5mm) needles

notions
Darning needle
Sewing machine or sewing kit
1 or 2 pairs of old jeans
4 pieces of card measuring 9in by 8 in (22cm by 20cm) to strengthen the sides (optional)
1 piece of card 8in by 8in (20cm by 20cm) to strengthen the base (optional)

size
Each panel is 9in by 8in (22cm by 20cm)

gauge
7 sts and 21 rows over 4in (10cm) square over stockinette stitch using size 9 (5.5mm) needles when piece is pinned out and stretched into shape

pattern
Sides (make 4)
Cast on 30 sts.
Work 42 rows in st st, beginning with a knit row. (Note that the purl side is the right side.)
Bind off loosely and evenly.

making up

Darn in any loose ends. Pin out the pieces right side down (i.e., purl side down) on a padded surface or blocking board until they are 9in by 8in (22cm by 20cm). Spray with water, then cover with a damp cloth and press with a hot iron. Leave to dry and then unpin. Your pieces should be the same size as your cardboard lining pieces if you are using them.

Take the jeans and decide which pockets you want where on the inside of the box. Then, using your pieces of card as templates, cut four pieces of denim to line the box, adding on ½in (1cm) or so for space to hem. Cut two further pieces of denim using the base card as a template. These don't need pockets (in fact, pockets would be wasted) – use instead the expanse of a leg. For one of the base pieces you will need a larger edge to hem as this edge is tucked in – allow three to four times the normal allowance.

Sew together the four knitted sides (the slightly longer edges are the sides), keeping the purl side as the right side, and sew the pieces edge to edge to create a topless and bottomless cube shape. Now take the denim pieces and create the lining by sewing the pieces together. Use the nature of the denim to keep the lining interesting; for instance, use the waistband as a top edge, or let a fly lap over a side edge to create an uneven but attractive feature. Now slipstitch the knitted work to the lining at the top, matching the corner seams, with wrong sides together and right sides out.

If you are using a lining, insert the cardboard pieces into the sides. With a few choice stitches, stitch along the side seams of both the knitted work and the denim lining. The piece should now have quite a defined boxy shape. Take the smaller base piece of denim and pin into place, then slipstitch it to the knitted work. Finally, take the final piece of denim to use as the bottom inner lining and tuck it around the base piece of card and push into place. It should fit nice and snugly and will add the final stability of your new storage cube.

The tufts and strands of fabric incorporated into this yarn create a wonderfully lively texture once knitted up.

tip This box would be a great gift for a would-be knitter; simply place inside a few artisan yarns, some colourful needles, and a copy of this book!

tip Use the seams and edges of the jeans to make the hems of the box. It adds to the denim look and is one less hem to machine- or hand-sew. These heavier seams can be made up of four or five layers of denim, so you will need a steady hand. In fact this, is the perfect time to break out the thimble collection.

tip If your raggy-yarn knitting is one-sided, like here, as opposed to two-sided like a scarf, make the most of the yarn by trying to keep all the fronds on the 'right side' as you knit, or use a crochet hook to pull the fronds through to the side where they will show.

rainbow rags storage cube 37

fruit fizz
coasters

Here we take a traditional crocheted item and recreate it in modern cotton and citrus-bright colours.

In the 'olden days', the cotton used for crochet was extremely fine – more like sewing thread than the yarns available today. The finished work was as intricate and delicate as lace, and pieces such as collars or window panels took months if not years to complete. Today's chunkier cottons are just as good for creating crochet pieces, but they can now be created in an evening. And whereas the traditional crochet colour was white, today's crochet queen has a huge range of vibrant colours to choose from.

Doilies, coasters and glass covers are traditional crocheted items that I thought deserved a modern twist. What better way to keep ice-cold lemonades and fruit juices safe from pesky insects than crochet covers in acid lime green, clementine orange or the hue of homemade lemon squash?

This project is also a great way to start working with beads. The pattern has been adapted with four designs, each using different sizes and styles of beads. I have also given a variation on the basic pattern to create some bright coasters using ribbon bought by the yard from a haberdashery store.

Cotton is updated for the modern age in wonderfully fresh and lively colours.

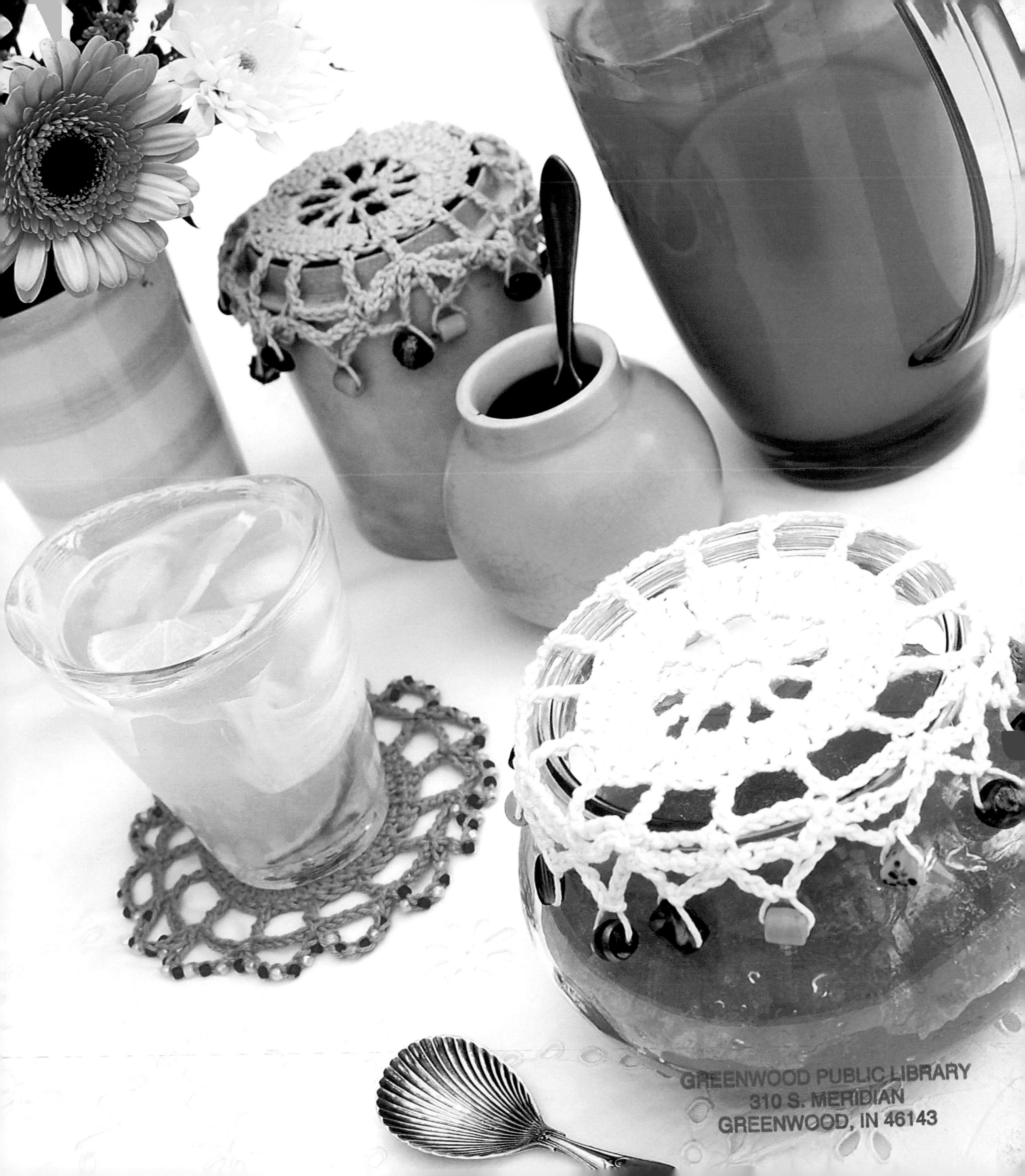

what you need and what you need to know...

yarn
For cotton covers: 1 x 1¾oz (50g) ball of fine-weight (4ply) cotton yarn

For ribbon coasters: 11yd (10m) satin ribbon ¼in (3mm) wide

hook
E4 (3.5 mm)

notions
Darning needle

Beading needle with large eye

Variation 1: 15 large glass beads

Variation 2: 30 medium beads in three different colours (90 in total)

Variation 3: 45 small beads in two different colours (90 in total)

Variation 4: 105 small beads in total in a mix of colours

size
Each coaster will be about 4½in (11cm) in diameter

gauge
Achieving an exact gauge is not essential here

pattern note In this pattern, tr denotes an American treble (see page 23). Those used to following British patterns should instead do a British double treble (see page 15). However, ch and ss mean the same, so slip that stitch and chain away with confidence.

Fine-weight (4ply) cotton has a lovely dry texture that gives a crisp, clear stitch definition.

basic pattern for beaded cotton covers
Make 10 ch and join with a ss to make a ring.

Round 1 6 ch (counts as first tr and 2 ch), (1tr into ring, 2 ch) 10 times, join with ss into 4th stitch of first chain, turn.

Round 2 4 ch (counts as first tr), 3 tr into first chain space, (1 tr into next tr, 3 tr into next chain space) 10 times, ss to top of 4 ch at beginning of round, turn.

Round 3 9 ch (counts as first tr and 5 ch), miss 3 st, (1 tr into next tr, 5 ch, miss 2 tr) 14 times, ss to 4th stitch of 9 ch at beginning of round, turn.

Round 4 (7 ch, ss into next tr) 15 times, turn.

Round 5 (9 ch, ss into 7th st) 15 times, fasten off yarn.

Variation 1 (see p. 39 top and bottom)
Thread 15 large glass beads onto the yarn before starting work.

Work as for basic pattern until end of round 4.

Round 5 (4 ch, 1ch taking in a bead, 4 ch, ss into 7th st) 15 times, fasten off yarn.

Variation 2 (see p. 41 bottom right)
Thread medium beads onto the yarn in batches of 6 in alternating colours before starting.

Work as for basic pattern until end of round 4.

Round 5 (4 ch, take one lot 6 beads and form a loop of them close to the hook, fasten loop off with 1 ch, 4 ch, ss into 8th st) 15 times, fasten off yarn.

Variation 3 (see p. 41 middle left)
Thread 90 small beads onto the yarn in two alternating colours before starting. Work as for basic pattern until end of round 3.

Round 4 (2 ch, work 3 ch taking a bead into each st, 2 ch, ss into next tr) 15 times.

Round 5 (3 ch, work 3 ch taking a bead into each st, 3 ch, ss into 7th st) 15 times, fasten off yarn.

Variation 4 (see p. 39 middle)
Thread 105 small beads onto the yarn in alternating colours before starting. Work as for basic pattern until end of round 3.

Round 4 (2 ch, work 7 ch taking a bead into each st, 2ch, ss into next tr) 15 times, fasten off yarn.

pattern for ribbon coasters (see p. 41 middle right)
Work as for basic pattern to end of round 2, then:

Round 3 (7 ch, ss into 5th st) repeat to end, fasten off.

making up
Darn in any loose ends. Cover the pieces with a damp cloth and press gently with a warm iron, pulling out the beads to create a droplet shape and ensuring that any loose chain stitches are pressed flat.

Always keep an eye out for jars of old beads in vintage stores to liven up your knitted and crocheted pieces.

tip When working with beads, keep enough yarn loose for the beads to travel down and not interfere with your hands. Similarly, ensure you choose beads with a large enough central hole for the yarn to pass through smoothly.

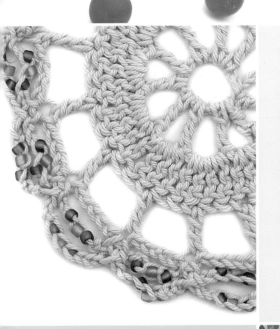

The ribbon variations of the coaster (shown right) have a lovely silky sheen to them. You can buy such ribbon by the yard, so you will have a whole rainbow of colours to choose from.

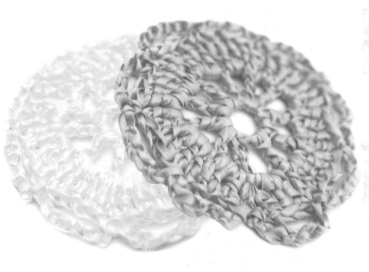

tip This pattern could easily be enlarged to create placemats and beautiful cake doilies. Try matching the colour to the occasion, such as red for Christmas, pink for Valentine's Day, or yellow for Easter.

bubbles & bobbles
cushion

This large floor cushion adds a little lamby softness to a fashionably modern home.

Beautiful, bubbly, bobbly bouclé yarn is full of texture. The new family of bouclé yarns offers 'daddy' types (really chunky yarns full of huge loops); 'mummy' versions (more refined and silky, with the addition of ribbon tufts); and 'kiddy' types (these have fun textures and colours, some with glitter).

When I spotted this chunky 'daddy' woollen bouclé, I couldn't get the image of a shearling out of my head, and imagined knitting up a large sheepskin blanket to snuggle under. However, the two-ball rule of this book doesn't allow for the making of king-size throws, so I had to scale down my ambitions to this large, huggable floor cushion.

The pattern itself could not be more simple – it is just a square, after all. However, this design features the dropped-stitch technique. Yes – the technique that breaks the cardinal rule of knitting and requires you to drop the stitches you have just spent all evening creating. This is not knitted vandalism, however: these stitches look amazing when woven through with other pieces of knitted work or, as here, with satin ribbons.

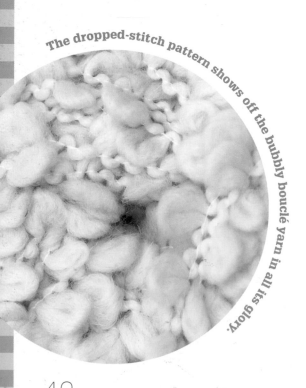

The dropped-stitch pattern shows off the bubbly bouclé yarn in all its glory.

what you need and what you need to know...

yarn
2 x 3½oz (100g) balls bulky-weight (chunky) bouclé yarn

needles
1 pair size 17 (12mm) needles

notions
Darning needle
24in (60cm) square cushion inner
Piece of toning fabric (we used fleece) 25½in by 49in (65cm by 125cm)
Sewing kit
60in (1.5m) of satin ribbon in toning shades in widths of 1¼in, ½in and ¼in (3cm, 1cm and ½cm)

size
20in (50cm) square (24in/60cm when stretched)

gauge
6 sts and 9 rows to 4in (10cm) square over dropped stitch pattern using size 17 (12mm) needles

tip When using a chunky bouclé like this, you need to be careful that those lovely loops don't get stuck and cause uneven tension in the knitting. Simply ensure that you don't have too much slack going around the needle and keep the tension of each stitch firm.

pattern
Cast on 30 sts loosely.
Row 1 Purl
Row 2 (RS) Knit.
Work 45 rows in st st as set.
Now start drop-stitch pattern.
Next row K2, slip next 2 sts off needle and use your fingers to unravel the knitting all the way down the piece of work to create a 'ladder'. Repeat this knit 2, slip 2 procedure until only 2 sts remain. Knit these 2 sts.
Next row (p2, cast on 2 sts over dropped sts) 7 times, p2.
Bind off evenly.

making up

Darn in any loose ends. Pin out the knitting onto a padded surface or blocking board to form the correct square shape. Cover with a damp cloth, press gently with a hot iron and leave to dry completely. Make the cushion by folding the fabric in half, right sides together. Sew along the two middle sides, leaving the top open. Turn right sides out. Either add a zipper or button edging, or add a cushion inner and slipstitch closed.

Take the ribbon and weave through the ladders, under and over the yarn. Add interest by adding a piece of ribbon crosswise, weaving under and over the yarn and ribbons. Pin all ribbons into place, leaving enough spare at each end for adjustments in length when sewing into place. Pin the knitted piece onto the cushion cover with the inner already in place, adjusting the ribbon pieces to fit. Now slipstitch the knitted piece carefully into place, sewing in ribbon ends as you go.

The bubbles and loops of bouclé yarn create a unique texture.

tip When dropping stitches, you may find it useful to lay the work flat to ensure all the stitches drop correctly. If you find it difficult to free the bubbles and loops, use a crochet hook to help pull the stitches through.

bubbles & bobbles cushion

kids

It is very satisfying to make items for babies and children: these things tend to be small so don't take long to make (heirloom blankets excepted!), and it is priceless to watch a child's face light up when she or he is presented with something made specially for them.

These items are perfect for creating with gourmet yarns, precisely because they are small and therefore use less yarn. You could use a yarn that is too precious and pricy to make something huge enough for a strapping man, or you could try some of the more eye-catching yarns that are best used in small quantities for maximum effect.

In this section, we have projects for children of all ages. For babies, we have a baby bonnet featuring variegated merino trimmed with fake fur. The girl's version has a hippyish tie-dye effect – perfect for your flower child – while the boy's version takes on a camouflage effect. I have also used lighter-than-air mohair for some tiny baby slippers, with many suggestions for embellishments to make them truly unique. For toddlers, there is a cheerful capelet in bright, chunky wool to give your little one some winter warmth, and a funky gilet in outrageous eyelash yarn. Finally, for children of all ages, I have used the strokeable texture of bouclé yarn to make some colourful animal characters.

fun-fur
baby bonnet

I love a baby in a bonnet; the ear-flaps that tie under the chin frame a sweet little face as well as keeping a child's ears warm and cosy.

One of the most useful new styles of yarn belongs to the furry family. These are yarns that when knitted or crocheted transform from a feathery strand into a piece of fake-fur fabric. The yarns can be used in a sophisticated way in muted or rich natural shades, or used in a more fun way in brighter hues. I think these yarns are best used in small quantities, as trimmings around collars and cuffs, or perhaps for a fun accessory such as a muff.

This bonnet is easy to create in simple crochet. The main part is crocheted in a colourful variegated merino yarn, while the use of a fake-fur trim turns it from a plainly made item into a special and covetable one. The bonnet has been designed with a wide-open front, as some babies don't like things too tight and close into their face, but the ear-flaps will keep them cosy and warm in the colder months.

Girls will love the pink version, while for boys I've chosen a more typically masculine khaki-toned yarn partnered with a chocolate fun fur to create a cosy trapper's hat – just don't call him sweet…

This yarn crochets up into a colourful and fun hippy-dippy chic fabric.

46

what you need and what you need to know...

yarn
A: 1 x 1¾oz (50g) ball of light-weight (DK) merino wool in variegated pattern

B: 1 x 1¾oz (50g) ball of bulky-weight (chunky) fake-fur yarn

hooks
1 size G6 (4mm)

1 size K10½ (6.5mm)

notions
Darning needle

Small amount of padding for bobbles

size
To fit a baby of around 9 to 18 months; when laid flat, flaps together, bonnet is 8¼in (21cm) wide and 10¼in (26cm) from crown to flap

gauge
10dc and 5 rows to 2in (5cm) square using yarn A and G6 (4mm) hook

safety note The under-chin ties should only be used on bonnets under adult supervision. If you prefer, the bonnet works just as well without them.

pattern note This bonnet is made in one piece, which means no sewing up. The crown is made working in the round, and then straight rows create the shape of the hem and the ear-flaps. The fur edging is simply a row of crochet in a show-stopping yarn.

Fake-fur yarn makes a great trimming for a crocheted garment

pattern

Crown
Using the smaller hook and yarn A, make 3 ch and join with a ss to make a ring.

Round 1 3 ch (counts as first dc), 11 dc into ring, join with ss into 3rd ch of first dc, 3 ch, turn.

Round 2 2 dc into each dc, join with ss, 3 ch, turn.

Round 3 (1 dc, 2 dc into next dc) 11 times, 1 dc, ss, 3 ch, turn.

Round 4 (1 dc into next 2 dc, 2 dc into next dc) 11 times, 1 dc, ss, 3ch, turn.

Round 5 (1 dc into next 3 dc, 2 dc into next dc) 11 times, 1 dc, ss, 3 ch, turn.

Round 6 (1 dc into next 5 dc, 2 dc into next dc) 9 times, 1 dc, ss, 3 ch, turn.

Rounds 7 and 8 1 dc into each dc, ss, 3 ch, turn.

Round 9 1 dc into next 32 dc, 2 dc into next dc, 1 dc into next 32 dc, ss, 3 ch, turn.

Round 10 1 dc into 3rd ch, 1 dc into each dc, ss, cut yarn and tie off.

Ear-flaps
Row 11 Rejoin yarn to work, 18 dc in from back seam, 3ch, then work 1 dc in next 36 dc, 3 ch, turn.

Row 12 1 dc into 5th ch from hook (2nd dc) and work 1 dc in next 33 dc, 3 ch, turn.

Row 13 Again starting 5ch from hook, work 1 dc in next 32 dc, 3 ch turn.

Row 14 Again starting 5 ch from hook, work 1 dc in next 30 dc, 3 ch, turn.

Row 15 Again starting 5 ch from hook, work 1 dc in next 28 dc, 3 ch, turn.

***Row 16** Starting 4 ch from hook, work 1 dc in next 11 dc, 3 ch, turn.

Row 17 Starting 5 ch from hook, work 1 dc in next 9 dc, 2 dc in next, 3 ch, turn.

Row 18 Starting 4 ch from hook, work 1 dc in next 10 dc, 3 ch, turn.

Row 19 Starting 5 ch from hook, work 1 dc in next 8 dc, 2 dc in next, 3 ch, turn.

Row 20 Starting 5 ch from hook, work 1 dc in next 8 dc, 3 ch, turn.

Row 21 Starting 5 ch from hook, work 1 dc in next 7 dc, 3 ch, turn.

Row 22 Starting 5 ch from hook, work 1 dc in next 6 dc, 3 ch, turn.

Row 23 Starting 5 ch from hook, work 1 dc in next 5 dc, 3 ch, turn.

Row 24 Starting 5 ch from hook, work 1 dc in next 4 dc, 3 ch, turn.

Row 25 Starting 5 ch from hook, work 1 dc in next 3 dc, cut yarn and pull through to tie off.

Now work other ear-flap to match from *, rejoining the yarn across the back and leaving a space of 6 chs from the start of the other ear-flap.

Edging
With WS facing and larger hook, attach yarn B to the middle of the back. Ch 2 and work a hdc row of fur yarn all the way around the edge of the bonnet, across flaps, front and back. When back at the middle of the back, ss the final hdc to the first. Cut yarn and tie off.

pattern note In this pattern, dc denotes an American double crochet and hdc an American half double crochet. Those used to following British patterns should instead do a British treble and half treble (see pages 15 and 23).

Under-chin straps

Using the smaller crochet hook and yarn A, attach yarn to bottom of right ear-flap, inside the fur edging. Work 63 ch, then, to create the ball ending, work 11 dc into 3rd ch from hook, ss to create a ring, 3 ch, turn.

Next row 1 dc into each dc, 3 ch, turn. (For a larger ball as in the pink bonnet, repeat this row.)

Next row 1 dc into 5th st from hook, (miss a dc, then dc into next) four times. Stuff the little ball with wadding or a scrap of toning fabric.

Miss 1 dc, then 1 dc into next st, join with a ss and pull tight. Cut the yarn and then darn this end into the ball well, ensuring that the bound-off end is nice and tight.

tip When darning in the ends of the fur yarn, don't try to darn in the full fur. Instead, snip off the strands and work in just the master thread. This makes it much easier to hide the ends of the bulky yarn.

tip If you prefer not to have a crocheted bobble, then use a double thickness of yarn for the chin tie to add a little more weight. Instead of a bobble, you could add a pom pom made in the fur yarn to keep the fabulously furry theme.

This variegated yarn in greens and khakis creates a camouflage effect when crocheted, for a more boyish variation.

knitty kitty
backpack

This colourful character is both huggable and useful; the kitty makes a backpack for a child to take on a fun day out.

This cute knitty kitty was designed to show off the unique texture of a twisted bouclé yarn. Bouclé is ideal for creating a double-sided fabric (that is, one where both sides are the same rather than having a right side and a wrong side), and is best used with a very simple stitch. This pattern is worked entirely in seed stitch (knit 1, purl 1); this bumpy stitch adds even more depth to the work. The backpack can be lined with a toning fabric for extra strength.

The backpack design can be adapted to create the friendly lion pyjama case (see pages 54–55). The lion has a mane made from loops of yarn oddments. Both projects are easily made in an evening or two.

The kitty backpack is made in three pieces: the front and back are identical, and are knitted from the bottom (the cat's 'chin') up. The gusset of the bag, which gives it some depth and storage capacity, is made separately and stitched into place. The pyjama case doesn't need such depth, so is made without the gusset.

The texture of bouclé makes it perfect for items designed for stroking like a pet.

what you need and what you need to know...

yarn
2 x 1¾oz (50g) balls of medium-weight (aran) bouclé yarn or light-weight (DK) bouclé yarn (used double throughout)

needles
1 pair size 9 (5.5 mm) needles

notions
Darning needle

Scissors

for backpack:
3 buttons for eyes and nose

2 buckles for straps

60in (150cm) of ribbon to fit buckle width

Contrast yarn for mouth and tongue

Button or toggle for closure

Piece of fabric 20in by 20in (50cm by 50cm) for lining (optional)

Wadding for ears (optional)

for pyjama case:
2 buttons for eyes

Yarn oddments for mane and embroidery

Snapper or button for opening (optional)

size
About 10½ by 9in (27 by 23cm)

gauge
13 sts and 18 rows to 4in (10cm) square over seed stitch using size 9 (5.5mm) needles

Bouclé is great for making items that lie next to the skin. You could use it for a cosy Russian hat, with the yarn mimicking the look of astrakhan.

pattern

Front and back (make 2)
Cast on 15 sts.

Row 1 Establish seed stitch pattern: (k1, p1) to last st, k1.

Row 2 Inc 1 (this will be a k st), (p1, k1) 7 times, inc 1 (this will be a p st), k1. 17 sts. Cont in seed stitch pattern and increase 1 stitch at each end of every row until there are 29 stitches.

Work 3 rows in seed stitch with no shaping.

Work 2 further rows of seed stitch, increasing 1 st at each end of each row. 33 sts.

Now work 20 rows of seed stitch with no shaping.

Row 34 Dec 1 at each end of row, then work 4 rows with no shaping. 31 sts.

Row 39 Dec 1 at each end of row, then work 2 rows with no shaping. 29 sts.

Row 42 Dec 1 at each end of row. * 27 sts.

Shape right ear
Row 43 K2tog, patt 17, turn, bind off 11 sts, patt to end, then work on these 7 sts. Work 3 rows

Next row **Patt 5, patt2tog. 6 sts. Work 1 row in seed stitch.

Next row Patt 4, patt2tog. 5 sts. Work 1 row in seed stitch.

Next row Patt 3, patt2tog. 4 sts. Work 2 rows in seed stitch.

Next row Patt2tog, patt 2. 3 sts. Work 1 row in seed stitch

Next row Patt2tog, patt 1. 2 sts. Work 1 row in seed stitch. P2tog, pull yarn through and cut off. **

Shape left ear
With RS facing, rejoin yarn and work to end in seed stitch.

Next row Patt2tog, patt to end. 7 sts. Work two rows, then repeat from ** to **.

Gusset
Cast on 2 sts.

Work 4 rows in k1, p1 seed stitch.

Next row *** Inc 1, patt to end. 3 sts. Work a further 10 rows in seed stitch*** Repeat from *** to *** 3 times more. 6 sts.

Next row Inc 1 st at beg of next row (7 sts) and then work 41 rows in seed stitch without shaping.

Next row ****k2tog, patt to end. 6 sts. Work a further 10 rows in seed stitch**** Repeat from **** to **** three times more. 3 sts.

Next row K2tog, patt to end. 2 sts. Work 4 rows straight with no shaping and then bind off.

tip To make the kitty's features, I used buttons for the eyes and nose, with the mouth sewn on in contrasting yarn and the tongue crocheted in pink cotton (3 ch, join with ss, 7 dc into ring, tie off). Alternatively, you could also cut the eyes and nose out of felt and embroider some whiskers.

Making up

Darn in any loose ends. Steam all pieces lightly with a damp cloth and hot iron, being very careful not to press on the knitting as this will flatten the pattern. Block the pieces into shape and leave to dry completely.

For the straps, cut two 20in (50cm) pieces of ribbon and two 10in (25cm) pieces. Attach the long pieces of ribbon to either side of the top opening of the back piece. Attach the shorter pieces (with buckle in place) to the bottom corner curve of the face. Sew the ribbon straps securely.

If using a lining, use the knitted pieces as templates to cut the lining pieces from the fabric. Sew the lining pieces together, with the right sides together (leaving the top unseamed). Then stitch the three knitted pieces together to form the bag, leaving the area between the ears unstitched to form the bag's opening. Insert the lining into the bag and slipstitch into place. You can use stuffing to form the kitty ears into a more three-dimensional shape. Once the wadding is in place, stitch across the bottom of the ear to follow the curve of the face and keep the padding in place.

After making up, sew a button or toggle in the middle of the back piece. Create a small corresponding loop in the middle of the front piece. You can use a piece of thin ribbon or simply use a small plaited piece of yarn and then sew firmly onto the piece. For a 1½in (3cm) button, allow a 2in (5cm) loop.

tip When sewing on the gusset, pin an end to each ear, then pin the middle of the gusset to the bottom of the face. Then pin in the middle of the gaps. Continue in this way until the gusset is entirely pinned. This ensures that the gusset is evenly placed around the face.

loopy lion pyjama case

pyjama case pattern

Work 2 pieces for the front and back as for the backpack until *: work one piece in yellow yarn and the other in brown.

When you reach *, patt 6, bind off centre 15 sts, patt to end, bind off.

making up

Press pieces lightly. Gather all your oddments of yarn to create a looping mane around the face (the yellow piece). Take the yarn, thread it into a darning needle, and pass through the knitted work and then back again leaving a loop. Knot the loop to keep it secure on the 'face' side. Continue in this manner until the whole face is surrounded by a border of loops for the mane.

Sew on brown buttons for eyes, and stitch on a nose and mouth (and perhaps some fierce teeth too).

Sew the pieces together, leaving a 6in (15cm) gap at the middle top (between the imaginary ears). Leave the gap free for younger children or add a snapper or button for an older child.

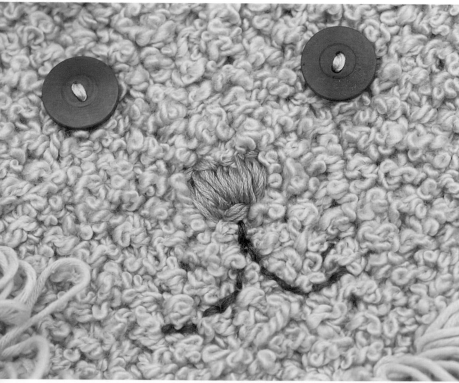

tip If time is short, you can create a cheat's mane. Buy a long length of upholstery fringing from your local haberdashery story in a leonine gold. Starting 2in (5cm) in from the edge, stitch the fringing into place in a long snaking circle to frame the face. When you reach the start point, continue in the snaking swirl ½in (1.25cm) behind the first row.

tip Make sure the button features are sewn on tightly so they're not worked loose and swallowed accidentally.

super-soft
slippers

Fine, gauzy, brushed mohair is used to create an adorable little pair of heirloom baby slippers in softest pink.

Mohair is a beautiful yarn to use for babies' items. The lightness and softness of mohair fabric means that it won't irritate a baby's skin. The gorgeous, delicate colours the yarn comes in makes it perfect for special garments that you will want to keep as mementos and heirlooms long after your little one has grown out of them.

The slippers shown here feature a feminine little ruffle. The addition of the simple frill turns the pair of feather-soft creamy shoes into little clouds – well, I think most babies are angels. However, I have provided a basic pattern, without the frill. You can then work variations on the basic pattern to produce a whole shoe shop's worth of different colours and textures. I have offered ideas for four other versions (see pages 58–59). The pom poms and animal faces make fun additions on little shoes that are perfect for a baby boy or girl. Little pink shoes with roses are just for girls, while the version with the star is just right for the little star in your life. I've used two strands of fine-weight (4ply) mohair, but the same pattern can be used using a single strand of heavier-weight yarn.

Mohair has a barely-there quality that makes finished items as light as a feather.

what you need and what you need to know...

yarn

1 x ⅞oz (25g) ball of fine-weight (4ply) mohair yarn (used double throughout) or 1 x ⅞oz (25g) ball of a fine-weight (4ply) silk-and-mohair mix

needles

1 pair size 5 (3.75mm) needles

notions

Darning needle

2 small buttons

Small stitch holder

Sewing kit

for pom pom variation: scrap of contrasting yarn and pom pom-making kit

for little stars variation: lurex yarn and D3 (3mm) crochet hook

for animal faces variation: scrap of contrasting yarn and thread for embroidery

for roses variation: scraps of pink and green yarn

size

4½in (11cm) from heel to toe (should fit a 6-month-old)

gauge

5.5 sts and 8 rows to 1in (2.5cm) square over stockinette stitch using size 5 (3.75mm) needles (using the fine yarn double and heavier-weight yarn singly)

This yarn creates a beautifully airy texture with a soft haze of colour.

basic slipper pattern

Left slipper

Cast on 24 sts.

Row 1 (WS) Inc 1, k12, m1, k12, inc 1. 27 sts.

Row 2 (RS) K13, m1, k1, m1, k13, inc 1. 30 sts.

Row 3 K14, m1, k3, m1, k13, inc 1. 33 sts.

Row 4 K14, m1, k5, m1, k14, inc 1. 36 sts.

Row 5 K15, m1, k7, m1, k14, inc 1. 39 sts.

Row 6 K15, m1, k9, m1, k15, inc 1. 42 sts.

Row 7 K16, m1, k11, m1, k15, inc 1. 45 sts.

Row 8 K16, m1, k13, m1, k16, inc 1. 48 sts.

Row 9 Knit to end, inc 1. 49 sts.

Row 10 (k1, p1) to last st, k1.

This row establishes seed stitch pattern. Repeat this row a further 8 times.

Shape instep

Row 19 (WS) Keeping k1, p1 seed stitch pattern correct, work 29 sts, k2tog, turn.

Row 20 (RS) S1, k9 (s1, k1, psso), turn. 47 sts.

Row 21 S1, p9, (s1, p1, psso), turn. 46 sts.

Row 22 S1, k9 (s1, k1, psso), turn. 45 sts.

Row 23 S1, p9, (s1, p1, psso), turn. 44 sts.

Row 24 S1, k9 (s1, k1, psso), turn. 43 sts.

Row 25 S1, p9, (s1, p1, psso), turn. 42 sts.

Row 26 S1, k9 (s1, k1, psso), turn. 41 sts.

Row 27 S1, p9, (s1, p1, psso), turn. 40 sts.

Row 28 S1, k9 (s1, k1, psso), turn. 39 sts.

Row 29 S1, p9, (s1, p1, psso), turn. 38 sts.

Row 30 S1, k9 (s1, k1, psso), turn. 37 sts.

Row 31 S1, p9, (s1, p1, psso), work in seed stitch pattern to the end. 36 sts.

Shape strap

Row 32 (RS)* Patt in seed stitch for 8 sts. Put these stitches onto a stitch holder. Bind off 4 sts in seed stitch, k2tog, bind off this stitch and 8 sts across the front of the shoe, k2tog and bind off this stitch and 4 further sts in seed stitch, then work 8 sts in seed stitch to end. This will leave the middle of the shoe, across the instep, bound off.

Row 33 (WS) K8, cast on 12 sts.

Row 34 (RS) K20. Now take the 8 sts on the stitch holder with the point of the needle towards the back seam of the shoe. Knit across these 8 sts. Then cast on 3 sts. 31 sts.

Row 35 (WS) K28, yo, k2tog, k1. 31 sts..

Row 36 (RS) Knit to end.**

Bind off loosely and evenly.

For right shoe, repeat as for left shoe, reversing shaping of the strap.

knitting note Use 2 strands of the mohair throughout. Knit through both strands for each stitch.

pattern note The slippers are knitted in one piece, using short rows for shaping (see page 20). The soles of the slippers are knitted in garter stitch, the sides and toe in seed stitch, and the upper in stockinette. The strap is made in garter stitch, secured with a little button. A yarnover forms the buttonhole.

making up

Darn in any loose ends. Steam the knitting gently with an iron – neither seed stitch nor mohair enjoy being squashed, so a good blast with a steam iron should do the trick. Sew the two sides of the sole together using mattress stitch so the two edges sit flat together. Sew on buttons on the strap to correspond with the buttonholes.

frilled variation

Work as for Basic pattern to **

Next row Purl to end.

Inc row (k1, m1) to last st, k1.

Purl 1 row then repeat the increase row.

Purl 1 row, then bind off.

pom pom variation

Work as for Basic pattern.

Make two small pom poms (see page 24) using about half the normal amount of yarn to ensure they are not too full. Use the yarn used in the slipper and a contrast colour or colours to add interest. Tie off pom pom and then fluff up to make a 'demi' pom with a flat back suitable for stitching firmly onto the shoe.

little stars variation

Work as for Basic pattern, but for the row marked *, substitute a strand of lurex for a strand of mohair to give an extra sparkle to the slipper edge. Using lurex yarn and D3 (3mm) crochet hook, 3 ch, join with ss. Work into the centre of the loop, (1 hdc, 1 dc, 1 dtr, 1 dc) five times, join with ss and fasten off yarn. Use a contrasting embroidery thread or lurex yarn to stitch initials on to each star. Stitch each star securely onto the slippers.

animal faces variation

Work as for Basic pattern.

Using a contrast colour mohair or soft woollen yarn and D3 (3mm) crochet hook, 3 ch, join with ss, 3 ch. Work 11 dc into the centre of the loop, join with ss, turn, miss a st and work 5 dc into next st, miss a st, ss, miss a st and work a further 5 dc into next st, miss a st, ss, then fasten off yarn.

Use a contrasting embroidery thread to add eyes, nose, mouth, and so on to create a face.

roses variation

Work as for Basic pattern.

Leaves (make 2)

Cast on 1 st using green yarn.

Row 1 K1, inc 1. 2 sts.

Row 2 Inc 1, k2, inc 1. 4 sts.

Row 3 Inc 1, k4, inc 1. 6 sts.

Row 4 Knit.

Row 5 K2tog, k2, k2tog. 4 sts.

Row 6 K2tog twice. 2 sts.

Row 7 K2tog and tie yarn off.

Roses (make 2)

Cast on 15 sts using rose-pink yarn.

Row 1 Purl.

Row 2 (K1, M1) to last st, k1.

Row 3 P15, turn, k to end.

Row 4 Purl to end.

Bind off.

Roll rose piece to create a flower bud and then stitch layers together at base. Sew on leaf and attach securely to the top of the slipper front, with the leaf at a jaunty angle.

colourful
capelet

Knitted in one shaped piece, this cheerful capelet is the perfect garment for a little one on cooler days.

I designed this baby capelet when novice knitter friends were bemoaning ever knitting something 'proper' – something that they or their family members could actually wear. After all, there are only so many scarves in a knitter's repertoire, and once you have mastered tension, changing colours and perhaps a little shaping then it really is time to move onto something more challenging. This project is just the thing. The pattern is an easy introduction to shaping using short rows (see page 20) as well as by knitting stitches together. And the results are very impressive! The cosy hood is created by picking up stitches (see page 21), while the whole garment is enlivened by the addition of a few colourful pom poms.

Although the project is knitted using just under two balls of yarn, I do feel I have cheated a little by using this wonderful wool, which could have been made especially for the two-ball knitter. Each strand of the yarn is made up of two strands of soft woollen fleece in ever-changing, contrasting colours that are twisted together, so it's really like knitting with four balls (well, I won't tell anyone if you won't!).

This boldly coloured yarn is perfect for children's items and home furnishings.

what you need and what you need to know...

yarn
2 x 3½oz (100g) balls of bulky-weight (chunky)
two-ply multi-coloured wool

needles
1 pair size 11 (8mm) needles, plus an extra
needle the same size

notions
Darning needle
Stitch holder
Sewing kit
Pom pom-making kit
Scraps of contrasting and toning coloured yarns
to make pom poms
40in (1m) of grosgrain ribbon ¾in (15mm)
wide (optional)

size
14in (35cm) from neck to hem; hood is 6¼in (16cm)

gauge
10 sts and 15 rows to 4in (10cm) square over
stockinette stitch using size 11 (8mm) needles

pattern note The capelet is knitted in one
piece from the bottom up in stockinette stitch. The hood
is edged with a border that overextends to provide an
under-chin tie. The project also features picking up stitches
and a three-needle bind-off (see page 21 for more on these
techniques).

**This vibrant, chunky
wool will knit up
satisfyingly
quickly.**

pattern
Cast on 20 sts and knit 1 row.
Continuing in st st (next row purl), cast
on 5 sts at beg of next 6 rows. 50 sts.
Next row Cast on 28 sts.
Row 1 P8, turn, knit to end.
Next row P14, turn, knit to end.
Next row P20, turn, knit to end.
Next row Purl across all sts.
Next row Cast on 28 sts.
Next row K8, turn, purl to end.
Next row K14, turn, purl to end.
Next row K20, turn, purl to end. 106 sts.
Now work 4 rows st st with no shaping.
Row 1 K27, k2togtbl, k48, k2tog, k27.
104 sts.
Work 3 rows st st.
Row 5 K26, k3togtbl, k46, k3tog,
k26. 100 sts.
Purl next row and all even rows until
row 28.
Row 7 K25, k3togtbl, k44, k3tog, k25.
96 sts.
Row 9 K24, k3togtbl, k42, k3tog, k24.
92 sts.
Row 11 K23, k3togtbl, k19, k2tog, k19,
k3tog, k23. 87 sts.
Row 13 K22, k3togtbl, k37, k3tog, k22.
83 sts.
Row 15 K21, k3togtbl, k17, k2tog, k17,
k3tog, k20. 78 sts.
Row 17 K19, k3togtbl, k34, k3tog, k19.
74 sts.
Row 19 K18, k3togtbl, k32, k3tog, k18.
70 sts.
Row 21 K17, k3togtbl, k30, k3tog, k17.
66 sts.
Row 23 K16, k3togtbl, k28, k3tog, k16.
62 sts.
Row 25 K15, k3togtbl, k26, k3tog, k15.
58 sts.

Row 27 Cast off 3 sts, k10, k3togtbl, k24,
k3tog, k14. 51 sts.
Row 28 Cast off 3 sts, p10, p3tog, p22,
p3togtbl, p10. 44 sts.
Row 29 K1, k2togtbl, k7, k3togtbl, k18,
k3tog, k7, k2tog, k1. 38 sts.
Row 30 P1, p2tog, p5, p3tog, p16,
p3togtbl, p5, p2tog, p1. 32 sts.
Row 31 K1, k2togtbl, k4, k3togtbl, k12,
k3tog, k4, k2tog, k1. 26 sts.
Row 32 P1, p2tog, p2, p3tog, p10, p3tog,
p2, p2tog, p1. 20 sts.
Row 33 K1, k2togtbl, k3togtbl, k8, k3tog,
k2tog, k1. 14 sts.
Cut the yarn and put the 14 sts onto a
spare needle. Now with RS facing, rejoin
yarn and pick up 5 sts down left front
neck edge, then the 14 sts from spare
needle and finally the 5 sts down right
front edge. 24 sts.
Work 6 rows st st with no shaping.
Next row (WS facing) P7, inc 1, p10, inc
1, p7. 26 sts.
Work 20 rows st st with no shaping.
Next row Use three-needle bind-off to
bind off the hood: K13, then fold the work
knit-side out so both needles are next to
each other and each stitch sits next to a
corresponding stitch on the other needle.
Now use a third needle to knit together
one stitch from each needle, and then
cast off this stitch. This will give a nice
neat ridge along the centre of the hood.

Hood edging and ties
Cast on 30 sts, pick up and knit 20 sts
down each side of the hood and cast on a
further 30 sts. 100 sts.
Purl 3 rows.
Bind off in purl.

making up

Darn in any loose ends. Make some small pom poms (see page 24) using any left-over yarn from the project and any spare yarn in your wool basket. Fix them onto the hem of the capelet and also to the ends of the hoodie ties.

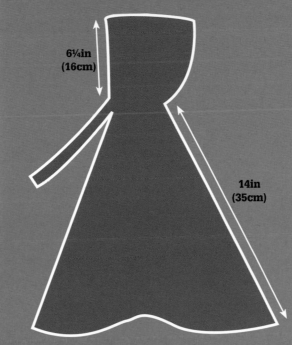

6¼in (16cm)

14in (35cm)

The capelet is knitted in stockinette stitch, with no edging on the bottom hem. This sometimes causes stockinette stitch to curl. However, the weight of this yarn, along with a good firm press, should ensure that the capelet lies flat, along with the extra weight of the pom poms.

tip An attractive way to finish off raw hems as used here is with a ribbon border. Simply stitch a ribbon inside the hem to add a little weight to an unfinished hem. I've used grosgrain ribbon here, which is slightly stiffer than regular satin ribbon and perfect for this type of hemming.

giddy
gilet

This little gilet shows off a wacky yarn in all its colourful and crazy glory – perfect for a dressing-up day.

Wild yarns are those that are a little bit crazy. Some are just a little wild, with perhaps a hint of glitter or a little colour variety, whereas others are certifiably crackers. Here is a recipe for the kind of wild yarn I'm talking about: take a ball of wool, add a sprinkling of glitter, a few handfuls of ripped ribbon, some wool tufts, a hint of cotton strands and mix up with a paintbox of colours and dye. The technical term for this type of uninhibited yarn is 'eyelash', which perfectly conjures up the way the fronds flutter out from a knitted piece of work.

Wild yarns are great for creating children's items, whether it's an extravagant-looking cosy hat and scarf or a fuzzy knitted friend. It might be a bit too outrageous for a whole garment – particularly on an adult – but is best appreciated on smaller knitted pieces.

This funky little gilet works just as well with a pair of jeans as it does with a fancy party dress. It is made in one piece, so no annoying shoulder seams get in the way of the fluffy knitted texture.

Eyelash yarn is fun and funky, full of crazy tufts and strands sticking out.

what you need and what you need to know...

yarn
2 x 1¾oz (50g) balls of bulky-weight (chunky) novelty eyelash yarn

needles
1 pair size 11 (8mm) needles

notions
Stitch holder
Darning needle
Sewing kit
40in (1m) ribbon in toning colour

size
To fit a three-year-old: 12½in (32cm) wide; 10½in (27cm) from hem to shoulder

gauge
9 sts and 7 rows to 4in (10cm) square over stockinette stitch using size 11 (8mm) needles

pattern note This piece is worked in stockinette stitch with a bottom edging of garter stitch. It is made in one piece, starting from the bottom of the back, and then working the left front from top to bottom after shaping the shoulders. You then rejoin the yarn to work the right front to match.

pattern

Cast on 32 sts.

Knit 5 rows in garter stitch (every row knit).

With next row purl, work 19 rows in st st.

Row 25 Cast off 3 sts at beg of next 2 rows. 26 sts.

Row 27 Cast off 1 st at beg of next 4 rows. 22 sts.

Row 31 Work 8 rows in st st.

Row 39 Divide for shoulder straps: knit 7, bind off centre 8 sts, knit to end, turn and work on these 7 sts only.* (You might want to put these 7 sts on a stitch holder.)

Row 40 P5, p2tog. 6 sts.

Work 2 rows st st.

Row 43 K2tog, k4. 5 sts.

Work 7 rows st st.

Row 51 Inc 1, knit to end. 6 sts.

Work 3 rows st st.

Repeat the last 4 rows twice more. 8 sts.

Row 63 Inc 1, knit to end, inc 1. 10 sts.

Work 3 rows st st.

Repeat the last 4 rows twice more. 14 sts.

Row 75 Inc 1 at each end of row. 16 sts.

Row 76 Cast on 3 sts, purl to end. 19 sts. (This forms the armhole and will match up with Row 25.)

Work 2 rows st st.

Row 79 Inc 1, knit to end. 20 sts.

Work 13 rows st st.

Row 93 Dec 1 st at the neck side of the next 3 rows, keeping st st pattern correct. 17 sts. (Make the decreases at least one stitch in from the edge to form a neat, curved edge.)

Row 96 Change to garter stitch (every row knit) and work 4 rows, decreasing 1 st at every neck edge. 13 sts.

Row 100 Bind off.

With WS facing, rejoin yarn and complete to match from *, reversing all shaping.

making up
Sew the side seams together. Place a damp cloth over the knitting and steam gently with an iron. Sew the ribbon to the front of the gilet as a tie.

This outrageous yarn creates a truly unique texture.

12½in (32cm)

10½in (27cm)

adults

When you have knitted something using a particularly special (and perhaps expensive) yarn, it is essential to have it on hand to garner compliments. That's why artisan yarns lend themselves so well to items that you might wear everyday – including eye-catching accessories such as scarves and hats, and glamorous garments such as shrugs and camisole tops. The beauty of many new-generation yarns is that they are so outstanding that the items you create with them could never be mistaken for being merely shop-bought.

We have used a stunning range of yarns for the projects in this section. For a stylish piece worn more for glamour than warmth, we have a beautifully fluid ribbon-yarn scarf. A slub wool with a magical thick-and-thin texture is used for a crocheted shrug in delicious summery colours. A simple camisole is given body-skimming drape through the use of slinky tube yarn. A truly luxurious mixture of yarns, including angora, cashmere and silk, is used for a striking two-tone effect bias-knit scarf. Finally, I have used a braid yarn (a hybrid of ribbon and bouclé that creates a towelling-type fabric) for a contemporary twist on the classic cloche hat of the 1920s.

running river
ribbon scarf

This sinuous river-inspired scarf is made from a slinky ribbon yarn. It forms a long wavy rope that curls in on itself.

There are many styles and variations of ribbon yarn, from delicate gauzy tape to heavy, thick and lustrous satin sashes. Often ribbon yarns feel silky and fluid in the hands – as this one did, which helped give me the watery inspiration for this wonderfully slinky scarf. Ribbon yarns often have a lustrous sheen to them, which adds to the fluidity of items knitted in them.

This ribbon yarn has a split personality: one half is silky ribbon dip-dyed to give stunning colour variations; the other is a cotton ribbon strip to give the work more weight and softness. This scarf is meant to be looped around a bare neck – more as a unique, stylish accessory than a winter warmer.

The scarf is knitted lengthways on a circular needle (buy the longest one you can find in the required size), which means casting on a lot of stitches to start with. Another technique used in this scarf is the use of a 'knitted in' tassel edging at each end. For this, you have to take a deep breath and unpick all your hard work to let the edges of the scarf work free, and then cut the ends to create a neat shape.

Ribbon yarn matches beautiful colour combinations with a wonderfully fluid texture.

what you need and what you need to know...

yarn
2 x 1¾oz (50g) balls of medium-weight (aran) ribbon yarn

needles
1 40in-long (100cm) size 10 (6mm) circular needle plus spare needle

size
About 60in (150cm) long (excluding fringe)

gauge
Achieving an exact gauge is not critical for the success of this pattern

pattern note The pattern is created with a series of decreases and increases that when used repeatedly gives the work a wavy edge at both sides.

tip When selecting a ribbon yarn, choose one that has a silky feel. Some ribbon yarns can be too stiff to create the fluid feel necessary for this project and are best left to tying presents.

pattern
Cast on 230 sts.
Row 1 K14, p1, k200, p1, k14.
Row 2 P14, k1, p200, k1, p14.
Row 3 K14, p1 (k2tog 5 times, yo 5 times) 20 times, p1, k14.
Row 4 As row 2
Repeat last 4 rows a further 4 times (20 rows knitted in total).

Make fringe
Cut yarn. Slip 20 sts onto spare needle,. Rejoin yarn and bind off 190 sts. Then slip needle out of remaining 20 sts.
Use your fingers to unravel the remaining stitches to create a fringe. This will give you a row of long, crinkly loops. The way the scarf is knitted will give the scarf a diagonal edge. Trim the edge of the fringe straight. Take each piece of ribbon and tie it to its neighbour to give the fringe an anchor and ensure the work doesn't unravel any further.
Complete the second fringe to match.

making up
Press very, very gently, covering the scarf with a damp cloth and a using warm iron. Be firm but don't crush the ribbon under the weight of iron. Then press the fringe.

tip Lay the work flat on a towel when making the fringe so you can pin out the loops of yarn as you work them free. This will make them easier to secure with knotting.

Ribbon yarns have a lovely drape to them, ideal for this glamorous scarf.

Using different types of ribbon tape creates different effects. In this variation (right), I knitted the scarf in a sari-ribbon fabric, which I like to imagine is a knitted evocation of the River Ganges.

simple
slub shrug

This pastel-coloured shrug is perfect to add a little summer-evening warmth to a party or prom dress.

Slubbed yarn is a marvellous mixture of chunky and slender fibres twisted together. This is the kind of yarn that on first glance shouldn't really work: tension surely flies out of the window when you are faced with working with something that can vary so drastically from elegantly fine to satisfyingly sturdy and back again. Any garment you make in slub yarn will be eye-catching simply because of its texture.

This summery little shrug is crocheted in five simple shaped pieces. It could easily be made in one evening when you're in need of an instant crafting fix. The loose texture of the stitches means that even though the yarn is cosy and chunky, the finished item doesn't look too heavy – and sun-kissed skin can still be seen peeking through the work.

If you want to break the two-ball rule, you could turn this into a little jacket by adding extra rows to both the sleeve and body length. The yarn I've used here is a soft slubbed wool that is hand-coloured in shades of peaches, cream and chocolate – quite delicious, I hope you will agree.

Slubbed yarns help to add textural interest to knitted and crocheted work.

what you need and what you need to know...

yarn
2 x 3½oz (100g) skeins of bulky-weight (chunky) slubbed yarn for small size (medium will take 3 skeins; large will take 4 skeins)

hook
O/P (12mm) hook

notions
Darning needle
Pins

size
Small to fit 34in bust; medium to fit 36–38in bust; large to fit 38–40in bust.

gauge
6 sc and 4 rows over 4in (10cm) square using O/P (12mm) hook

pattern note In this pattern, dc denotes an American double crochet. Anyone who is used to following British patterns should instead do a British treble (see pages 15 and 23).

The combination of thick and thin in this yarn creates a unique texture.

pattern

Back
Make 5 ch and join with ss into a ring, 3 ch, turn.

Round 1 Into the ring work 12 dc, ss into 3rd ch of foundation chain to join and create round, 3 ch, turn.

Round 2 1 dc into 3rd ch from hook, 2 dc into next 12 dc, ss to join, 3 ch, turn.

Round 3 2 dc into 3rd ch from hook, 1 dc in each of next 5 dc, (3 dc in next dc, 1 dc in each of next 5 dc) 3 times, ss to join, 3 ch, turn.

Round 4 2 dc in 3rd ch from hook, 1 dc in each of next 7 dc, (3 dc in next dc, 1 dc in each of next 7 dc) 3 times, ss to join, 3 ch, turn.

Round 5 2 dc in 3rd ch from hook, 1 dc in each of next 9 dc, (3 dc in next dc, 1 dc in each of next 9 dc) 3 times, ss into 3rd ch to join, 3 ch, turn.

Round 6 (medium and large sizes only) 2 dc in 3rd ch from hook, 1 dc in each of next 11 dc, (3 dc in next dc, 1 dc in each of next 11 dc) 3 times, ss into 3rd ch to join, 3 ch, turn.

Round 7 (large size only) 2 dc in 3rd ch from hook, 1 dc in each of next 13 dc, (3 dc in next dc, 1 dc in each of next 13 dc) 3 times, ss into 3rd ch to join, 3 ch, turn.
Now add width to the piece of work:

Next row (all sizes) 1 dc into next 10 (12:14) dc along the round, ch 3, turn.

Next row (all sizes) 1dc into next 10 (13:16) dc along the round. Cut yarn and tie off.
Now rejoin yarn to other corner of the work to add width to the other side of the piece, and repeat the last 2 rows.

Front pieces (make 2)
Make 4 ch.

Row 1 Work 6 dc into the first st of the chain (that is, the chain furthest from your hook), 3 ch, turn.

Row 2 1 dc in 3rd ch from hook, 2 dc into next 4 dc, 1dc, 3ch, turn.

Row 3 1 dc in 3rd ch from hook, 1 dc in next dc, (1 dc in next dc, 2 dc into next dc) three times, 1 dc in next 2 dc, 3 ch, turn.

Row 4 1 dc in 3rd ch from hook, 1 dc in next dc, (2 dc in next dc, 1 dc in next 2 dc) three times, 2 dc in next dc, 1 dc in next dc, 3 ch, turn.

Row 5 (medium and large sizes only) 1 dc in 3rd ch from hook, (2 dc in next dc, 1 dc in next 4 dc) three times, 2 dc in next dc, 3 ch, turn.

Row 6 (large size only) 1 dc in 3rd ch from hook, (2 dc in next dc, 1 dc in next 4 dc) four times, 3 ch.

Next row (all sizes) Now stop working around the round edge and work down the flat edge of the work (the sides of the dcs). Pick up 10 (13 for medium size, 16 for large size) dc along the width, ch3, turn.
Work a further 3 (3 for medium size, 4 for large size) rows along this edge with 1 dc in each dc. Cut yarn and tie off.

Sleeves (make 2)
Make 4 ch.

Row 1 Work 6 dc into the first st of the chain, 3 ch, turn.

Row 2 1 dc in 3rd ch from hook, 2 dc into next 4 dc, 1dc, 3 ch, turn.

Row 3 1 dc in 3rd ch from hook, 1 dc in next dc, (1 dc in next dc, 2 dc into next dc) three times, 1 dc in next 2 dc, 3 ch, turn.

Row 4 1 dc in 3rd ch from hook, 1 dc in next dc, (2 dc in next dc, 1 dc in next 2 dc) three times, 2 dc in next dc, 1 dc in next dc, 3 ch, turn.

Row 5 1 dc in 3rd ch from hook, (2 dc in next dc, 1 dc in next 4 dc) three times, 2 dc in next dc, 3 ch, turn.

Row 6 (medium and large sizes only) 1 dc in 3rd ch from hook, (2 dc in next dc, 1 dc in next 4 dc) four times, 3 ch.

Row 7 (large size only) 1 dc in 3rd ch from hook, (2 dc in next dc, 1 dc in next 5 dc) four times, 3 ch.

Next row (all sizes) Now stop working around the round edge and work down the flat edge of the work (the sides of the dcs). Pick up 13 (16 for medium size, 19 for large size) dc along the width, ch 3, turn.

Work a further 3 (4 for medium size, 5 for large size) rows along this edge with 1 dc in each dc.

Cut yarn and tie off.

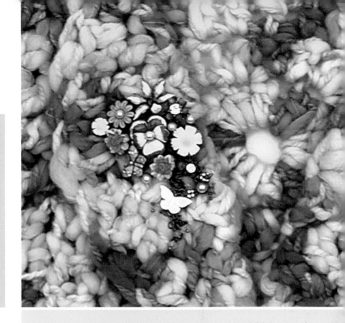

making up

Darn in any loose ends. Pin out the pieces on a board, shaping them to keep round edges round and squared-off edges square. Steam well and leave to dry. Pin the front pieces to the back and sew a 3¼in (8cm) shoulder seam (4in/10cm for medium size, 5¼in/13cm for large) from the edge to the neckline at each side. Pin the sleeve heads into place and sew a 3¼in (8cm) sleeve seam (4in/10cm for medium size, 5¼in/13cm for large), then stitch the sleeve head into place. Fold back the front round lapels, pin into place, iron, then add a stitch to hold in place. Rejoin the yarn to the front edge at the right side of the front and ch 3, pick up and place a dc into stitches around the body and work two rows to add length. If you want to turn the shrug into a jacket, then just keep going until you run out of yarn.

tip To add a touch of 1940s glamour to this shrug, add a pair of vintage brooches to the lapels, or decorate them with a couple of large buttons.

tip When you seam together pieces made in chunky wool, you might want to use a piece of lighter-weight yarn in a toning colour. If you use the chunky yarn, your seams might be lumpy and distort the shape of the garment.

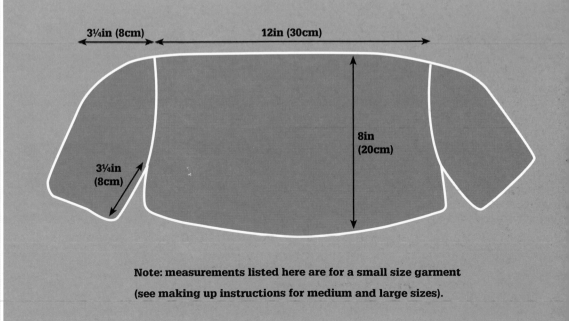

3¼in (8cm)   12in (30cm)

8in (20cm)

3¼in (8cm)

Note: measurements listed here are for a small size garment (see making up instructions for medium and large sizes).

corsage
camisole

The simple construction of this elegant camisole means that this is a project that even a novice could tackle.

The tape yarn used for this camisole is a variation of a ribbon yarn. It is a tape of jersey with a silky texture perfect for creating items that drape across the body. The tape yarn used here is quite chunky; finer tape yarns are available that are excellent for using in more delicate patterns. The defined nature of the yarn makes for interesting lace knitting, as every stitch is visible, while the fluid texture is perfect for sweaters and scarves.

This camisole captures the slinkiness of the tape yarn. The knitted-in straps allow it to be fitted exactly to size. The decorative flower corsage is made using smaller needles and is decorated with a smattering of buttons. It's good to have a flower pattern in your creative armoury to use as embellishments for your knitted work, and this one works just as well in any yarn.

The weight of this silky yarn makes the camisole hang beautifully.

what you need and what you need to know...

yarn
2 x 1¾oz (50g) balls bulky-weight (chunky) tape yarn

needles
1 pair size 16 (12mm) needles
1 pair size 5 (3.75mm) needles

notions
Darning needle
4 stitch holders
Sewing kit
To decorate corsage: 10 small buttons, 1 larger button

size
Finished garment will fit US size 6 (UK size 10)

gauge
9 sts and 11 rows to 4in (10cm) square over stockinette
stitch using size 16 (12mm) needles

pattern note The camisole is knitted in
stockinette stitch in one piece with a centre back seam.
Both straps are knitted using the main body of the yarn
rather than attached after the main piece is knitted. Using
such small needles to knit up the corsage may seem
strange after using chunky ones for the camisole. However,
this will make the flower stiff and hold its shape better. If
you find it awkward, try needles one or two sizes larger. The
flower is knitted in one piece creating 'petals' by knitting
a stitch and then passing a number of stitches of this off
the needle. They will hang in a little 'hammock' in the work
until you fasten them off by knitting the initial stitch again.

pattern

Camisole
Cast on 63 sts with the larger needles.
Work 18 rows in st st, beginning with a
knit row (Knit side is the RS).
Row 19 (RS) Bind off 3 sts at beg of next
2 rows. 57 sts.
Row 21 Dec 1 at each end of next 5
rows. 47 sts.
Rows 26 and 27 Work these two rows
without shaping.
Row 28 P2, put these 2 sts on a stitch
holder, bind off 3 sts and purl across the
row. 42 sts.
Row 29 K2, put these 2 sts on a stitch
holder, bind off 3 and then knit to end.
(These 2 lots of 2 stitches set aside on
stitch holders form the basis of the straps
at the back of the camisole.)
Row 30 Dec 1 at each end of next 4
rows. 29 sts.
Row 34 Purl.
Row 35 Dec 1 at each end of row. 27 sts.
Row 36 Purl.
Row 37 Dec 1 at each end of row. 25 sts.
Row 38 Purl.
Row 39 Dec 1 at each end of row. 23 sts.

Row 40 Purl.
Row 41 Knit 7 sts, turn, and work on
these stitches only.
Row 42 P2tog, p5. 6 sts.
Row 43 K4, k2tog. 5 sts.
Row 44 P2tog, p3. 4 sts.
Row 45 K2, k2tog. 3 sts.
Row 46 P2tog, p1. 2 sts
Keep these 2 sts on stitch holder (these
are the stitches from which the straps
are knitted).
Rejoin yarn to the work with WS facing.
Bind off centre 9 sts, and work second
side to match other, reversing all shaping.

Flower corsage
Cast on 51 sts using the smaller needles.
Rows 1 to 3 Knit.
Row 4 (K1, slip this st back onto the left-
hand needle and pass 8 sts over, knit the
first st again, K1) 5 times, k1.
Rows 5 to 7 Knit.
Pull yarn through remaining 6 sts, pull
tight and cut the yarn. Sew the largest
button into the centre of the flower and
then sew the little buttons on the petals,
like dew.

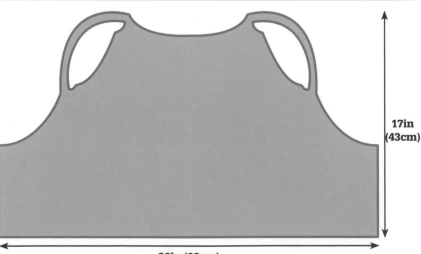

Tape yarn
creates a
knitted fabric
that is fluid
and silky.

26in (66cm)

17in
(43cm)

corsage camisole

tip Tape yarn is very silky and is a pleasure to knit with. I have also experimented with cutting the tape so you have a long, fraying flat piece of yarn. Try knitting the corsage in this frayed yarn for a different effect.

making up

Darn in any loose ends. Place the camisole right-side down, cover with a damp cloth and press with a hot iron. Sew the back seam of the camisole. Check again the length of the straps (the yarn is heavy and may stretch, so you should probably be conservative in the length of the straps). Adjust the length if necessary by knitting or unravelling a few rows. When satisfied, sew the straps into place. Place the corsage at the neckpoint where the two sides separate (there is usually a small gap left here, so disguise it with the corsage). Sew on securely. Add a couple of extra yarn loops sewn into the back to hang down like ribbons.

tip I am an enthusiast for recycling. No shirt is thrown away in my house without all buttons first being snipped off. This kind of project is great for using up salvaged buttons, as the corsage looks better with mismatched ones.

two-tone
twist scarf

This design takes a luxurious yarn and creates a scarf to drape around the neck, ensuring the soft opulence stays right next to your skin.

Today's knitters are a spoiled breed. In the dark days of yesteryear, the choice of yarn was basic wool, cotton or acrylic, with not a lot in between. A 1950s knitter would be knocked speechless on her kitten heels at the glorious array of yarns on offer these days. Luxury no longer means 100% pure new wool – wow! Today's premium yarns are truly extravagant. Not just cashmere, not just angora… they can be a heady mix of all the most luxurious yarns in the world.

The yarn we've used for this colourful scarf features an extraordinary mixture of wool, silk, cashmere, angora, alpaca, kid mohair and camel. If that weren't special enough, it is also hand-painted to give broad swathes of gently changing colour.

Knit on the bias, the scarf combines two softly variegated yarns in alternating two-row stripes to give it a sophisticated look that appears infinitely more complicated than it is (don't you just love it when that happens…). Knitting the scarf in garter stitch adds bulk and warmth.

This sumptuous yarn mix feels silkier than silk through the fingers.

what you need and what you need to know...

yarn
2 x 3½oz (100g) skeins of bulky-weight (chunky) variegated cashmere-mix yarn

needles
1 pair size 10 (6mm) needles

notions
Darning needle

size
45in (115cm) long by 6in (15cm) wide

gauge
14 sts and 28 rows to 4in (10cm) square over garter stitch using size 10 (6mm) needles

pattern note The scarf is knitted entirely in garter stitch. Alternate between the two balls of wool every third row to create the striped effect.

You can achieve striking colour-change effects with variegated hand-painted yarns such as this.

pattern
Cast on 3 sts with your first ball of yarn.
Row 1 K3, inc 1. 4 sts.
Row 2 Inc 1, k4. 5 sts.
Row 3 Join in the second ball of yarn, keeping the first joined to the piece. K5, inc 1. 6 sts.
Row 4 Inc 1, k6. 7 sts.
Row 5 Change back to the first ball of yarn, keeping the second joined to the piece. Continue in this way, swapping back and forth every third row. Now inc 1, k7, inc 1. 9 sts.
Row 6 Inc 1, k9. 10 sts.
Row 7 K10, inc 1. 11 sts.
Row 8 Inc 1, k11. 12 sts.
Row 9 K12, inc 1. 13 sts.
Row 10 Inc 1, k13, inc 1. 15 sts.
Row 11 K15, inc 1. 16 sts.
Row 12 Inc 1, k16. 17 sts.
Row 13 K17, inc 1. 18 sts.
Row 14 Inc 1, k18. 19 sts.
Row 15 Inc 1, k19, inc 1. 21 sts.
Row 16 Inc 1, k21. 22 sts.
Row 17 K22, inc 1. 23 sts.

Row 18 Inc 1, k23. 24 sts.
Row 19 K24, inc 1. 25 sts.
Row 20 Inc 1, k25, inc 1. 27 sts.
*Knit 4 rows.
Row 25 Inc 1, knit to last 2 sts, k2tog. 27 sts.
Knit 4 rows.
Row 30 K2tog, knit to end, inc 1. 27 sts.*
Repeat last 10 rows (from * to *) until 290 rows have been worked.
Knit 2 rows.
Row 293 K2tog, k25. 26 sts.
Row 294 K24, k2tog. 25 sts.
****Row 295** K2tog, knit to last 2 sts, k2tog. 23 sts.
Row 296 Knit to last 2 sts, k2tog. 22 sts.
Row 297 K2tog, knit to end. 21 sts.
Row 298 Knit to last 2 sts, k2tog. 20 sts.
Row 299 K2tog, knit to end. 19 sts.**
Repeat from ** to ** 2 times more. 7 sts.
Row 310 K2tog, k3, k2tog. 5 sts.
Row 311 K2tog, k3. 4 sts.
Row 312 K2 st, k2tog. 3 sts.
Bind off.

making up
Darn in any loose ends. Pin out the knitting on a padded surface or blocking board. You want to ensure the edges are square. Place a damp cloth over the knitting and steam gently with an iron. Leave to dry completely.

tip Make sure your ball of cheaper, plain-coloured yarn is the same weight and knits up to the same gauge as your luxury yarn, or your stripes will be uneven and the overall shape of the scarf will be distorted.

For a striking variation on this pattern, try using one ball of brightly coloured variegated luxury yarn teamed with a ball of plain yarn. This will really show off the bias knitting and the colour change of the main yarn, as well as being cheaper. Luxury yarns such as this are the caviar of the crafts world, so it makes sense to add a little sour cream to make it go further.

classic
cloche hat

This hat takes the classic cloche hat beloved of flappers in the 1920s, and updates it for the twenty-first century.

This yarn looks like luxurious towelling material with its loops of soft cotton.

Braid yarns are a hybrid of bouclé and ribbon, stitched together to form an exciting and quite unique yarn that is generally soft and sumptuous. It feels quite fine and light in the fingers, but actually knits up quite chunkily, so it's perfect for items where you want substance but not too much weight and bulk. It would be perfect for a summer evening wrap, or for cosying up on the beach at the end of a sea-splashed day.

The towelling-style fabric of this braid yarn reminded me of a vintage cover of *Vogue* magazine. I could imagine a poised model with artfully arched eyebrows staring out of the cover from beneath the brim of a chic cloche hat. These hats were fashionable in the 1920s, and were iconic of the flapper era. To wear a cloche hat correctly, it must be all but pulled right over the eyes, causing the wearer to peer out from beneath it.

This hat is knitted vertically on the crown and horizontally along the brim. The brim can be worn turned up, or pulled down to frame the face in true cloche fashion. A simple flower adds another flapper-era touch.

what you need and what you need to know...

yarn
2 x 1¾oz (50g) balls of bulky-weight (chunky) ribbon braided yarn

needles
1 pair size 11 (8mm) needles

notions
Darning needle
Sewing kit
Button or beads to embellish flower

size
12½in (32cm) from crown to brim; this hat should fit all sizes as the ribbing and the yarn make it stretchy

gauge
10 sts and 12 rows to 4in (10cm) square over stockinette stitch using size 11 (8mm) needles

pattern note The hat is knitted in two pieces: a crown that is worked in one piece with a side seam, and a brim that is knitted as one long piece and then stitched to the crown. Both pieces are knitted in a simple rib pattern to show off the beauty of the yarn.

This yarn combines the fluidity of ribbon yarn and the looped texture of bouclé yarn.

pattern

Crown
Cast on 63 sts.
Row 1 (RS) (k4, p1, k4) to end.
Row 2 (p4, k1, p4) to end. These 2 rows set the rib pattern.
Work a further 10 rows in rib pattern.
Row 13 K4, (p1, k3, k2tog, k3) 6 times, p1, k2, k2tog. 56 sts.
Row 14 P3, k1 (p7, k1) 6 times, p4.
Row 15 (k4, p1, k3) to end.
Row 16 P3 (k1, p2, p2tog, p3) 6 times, k1, p2, p2tog. 49 sts.
Row 17 K3, p1 (k6, p1) 6 times, k3.
Row 18 (p3, k1, p3) to end.
Row 19 K3 (p1, k2, k2tog, k2) 6 times, p1, k1, k2tog. 42 sts.
Row 20 P2, k1 (p5, k1) 6 times, p3.
Row 21 K3, p1 (k5, p1) 6 times, k2.
Row 22 P2 (k1, p1, p2tog, p2) 6 times, k1, p2tog, p1. 35 sts.
Row 23 K2, p1 (k4, p1) 6 times, k2.
Row 24 P2, k1 (p4, k1) 6 times, p2.
Row 25 K2tog (p1, k1, k2tog, k1) 6 times, p1, k2. 28 sts.
Row 26 P2, k1 (p3, k1) 6 times, p1.
Row 27 K1 (p1, k3), p1, k2.
Row 28 P2tog (k1, p2tog, p1) 6 times, k1, p1. 21 sts.
Row 29 K1 (p1, k2) p1, k1.
Row 30 K2tog (p2tog, k1) 6 times, p1. 14 sts.
Row 31 (p2tog) 7 times, pull yarn through and tie off, leaving a piece long enough to sew back seam.

Brim
Cast on 10 sts.
Row 1 (RS) (k2, p2) 2 times, k2.
Row 2 (p2, k2) 2 times, p2.
Repeat these last 2 rows until 92 rows worked in total.
Bind off in rib.

Flower
Cast on 30 sts.
Row 1 Knit.
Row 2 K2tog to end. 15 sts.
Row 3 Knit.
Row 4 (k2tog) 7 times, k1. 8 sts.
Row 5 Knit.
Row 6 (k2tog) 4 times. 4 sts.
Pull yarn through, cut and tie off tightly. With the end of the yarn, sew up the two sides to create a round piece of knitting.

I thought this cloche hat would look equally lovely in the fresh colours of spring.

making up

Lay the pieces right-side down on a board, cover with a damp cloth and iron gently with a hot iron. Don't press down; the steam should just breathe on the knitted work. Sew the back seam of the crown. Pin the brim to the crown and stitch into place. The two ends of the brim will meet on the front right of the hat, about 2½in (6cm) to the right of the centre point; this is where the flower will be attached, so it will hide the join. Don't worry if the brim ends don't meet exactly, or overlap, as they will be covered. Sew the flower into place, and then add the decoration of your choice – button, beads, or whatever else you fancy.

tip This hat will make the perfect showcase for a special button. The button I used on the pink hat was rather expensive – but it is made of shell and hard-carved.

tip On the green hat I added a cluster of glass beads as the centre of my flower. Thread the beads on a length of cotton and stitch the cluster to the flower. I chose to coordinate the colour of the beads with the yarn, but you could choose a contrasting shade for an extra burst of colour.

gifts

Gourmet yarns are the perfect choice when you are making
something as a special gift. Giving someone a present is a lovely
gesture anyway, but when you give someone an item that you
have crafted by hand especially for them, in a beautiful artisan
yarn, you will see real gratitude in their eyes.

In this section we present a range of projects that are fun to make
and even more fun to give. First up is a yarn that is show-stopper
perfect for celebrating a good friend's inner showgirl: glitzy lurex.
A dog-loving pal would appreciate dressing up their beloved pet
for walkies in a colourful linen jumper. Other yarns used in this
section are self-striping sock yarn (but not for socks, of course;
that would be far too obvious) and a combination of hazy, sheeny
ribbon yarn and crisp lurex for a glamorous hipster belt. Finally,
an ebullient friend should surely receive something created in a
crazy, wild yarn like the exuberant Bollywood bag.

pucker-up
purse

Here, a pair of Dali-esque luscious lips is transformed into a cosmetics bag perfect for the lipstick addict in your life.

If every type of yarn represented a place, then lurex would be Las Vegas: twinkly, bright, and a little bit trashy. A garment knitted from lurex would be uncomfortably scratchy, but this yarn comes into its own for creating glamorous accessories or for trimming outfits, adding glitz and shine when partnered with a softer yarn.

I took the inspiration for this purse pattern from Salvador Dali's legendary 'Mae West Lips' sofa. I chose to knit it in bright red, true to Mr Dali's vision. However, it would also make a great gift for a teenager when knitted in a blush pink (see page 93) and filled with glamorous new make-up.

The purse is knitted in stockinette stitch. The pouting effect of the lips is created with short rows; this gives the fabric a three-dimensional shape and a shapely outline. Short rows simply means knitting as normal but not to the end of the row; when you get to the part you want to 'plump', turn the knitting, slip a stitch so as not to create a hole, and knit back on yourself (see page 20 for more on this technique).

Lurex yarn has a lovely crunchy, firm texture, full of light and sheen.

what you need and what you need to know...

yarn

2 x 1¾oz (50g) balls of fine-weight (4ply) lurex yarn, used double throughout

needles

1 pair size 3 (3.25mm) needles

notions

Stitch holder

Darning needle

20in (50cm) square toning fabric for lining

7in (18cm) zipper

Sewing kit for hand sewing or sewing machine

Stuffing (optional)

size

Finished 'pout' is 8in (20cm) wide

gauge

26 sts and 40 rows to 4in (10cm) square over stockinette stitch using size 3 (3.25mm) needles

pattern note The front and back are different sizes, as the front piece will be padded to give it additional 'oomph'. When sewing the pieces together, pin first and then adjust pins around the edges until you get the best fit.

knit note The yarn is used double throughout; make sure that you knit through both strands of yarn for each stitch.

One of lurex yarn's best properties is its texture; when knitted using a smaller-gauge needle it creates a very firm fabric, ideal for items that will get a lot of wear and tear like these purses.

pattern

Front

Cast on 20 sts.

Row 1 Inc 1, k20, inc 1. 22 sts.

Row 2 and every even row until zip shaping Purl.

Row 3 Inc 1, k5, m1, k12, m1, k5, inc 1. 26 sts.

Row 5 Inc 1, k26, inc 1. 28 sts.

Row 7 Inc 1, k22, turn, ss, p15, turn, ss, knit to end, inc 1. 30 sts.

Row 9 Inc 1, k30, inc 1. 32 sts.

Row 11 Inc 1, k6, m1, k20, m1, k6, inc 1. 36 sts.

Row 13 Inc 1, k36, inc 1. 38 sts.

Row 15 Inc 1, k28, turn, ss, p17, turn, ss, knit to end, inc 1. 40 sts.

Row 17 Inc 1, k40, inc 1. 42 sts.

Row 19 Inc 1, k7, m1, k28, m1, k7, inc 1. 46 sts.

Row 21 Inc 1, k46, inc 1. 48 sts.

Row 23 Inc 1, k34, turn, ss, p19, turn, ss, knit to end, inc 1. 50 sts.

Row 25 Inc 1, k50, inc 1. 52 sts.

Row 27 Inc 1, k15, k2togtbl, k18, k2tog, k15, inc 1. 52 sts.

Repeat last 2 rows twice more, then purl 1 row.

Begin zip shaping

Row 33 K4 and working only on these sts, work 3 rows. Then cut yarn and place these sts on a stitch holder.

With RS facing, rejoin yarn to stitches and work on centre 44 sts. Purl 1 row to create a ridge.

Work 3 rows in st st and then bind off.

Cast on 44 sts and work 3 rows in st st, starting with a knit row.

Work 1 knit row to create a ridge, then place the sts on a stitch holder and cut yarn.

Rejoin yarn to remaining 4 sts and work 3 rows.

Next row Knit across these 4 sts, the 44 cast-on stitches, and then across the 4 sts held on the stitch holder. Work 2 rows in st st with no shaping.

Upper lip

Row 1 K2tog, k15, m1, k18, m1, k15, k2tog. 52 sts.

Row 2 and every even row until row 24 Purl.

Rows 3 and 5 As row 1.

Row 7 K2tog, k33, turn, ss, p18, turn, ss, knit to last 2 sts, k2tog. 50 sts.

Row 9 K2tog, k33, turn, ss, p16, turn, ss, knit to last 2 sts, k2tog. 48 sts.

Row 11 K2tog, k22, turn and work on these stitches, leaving remaining stitches on a stitch holder.

Row 13 K2tog, k18, k2tog. 20 sts.

Row 15 K2tog, k15, turn, ss, p13, turn, ss, knit to last 2 sts, k2tog. 18 sts.

Row 17 K2tog, k14, k2tog. 16 sts.

Row 19 K2tog, k10, turn, ss, p7, turn, ss, knit to last 2 sts, k2tog. 14 sts.

Row 21 K2tog, k12, k2tog. 12 sts.

Row 23 K2tog, k10, k2tog. 10 sts.

Row 24 Bind off 2 sts, p6, p2tog. 9 sts.

Bind off remaining stitches.

With RS facing, rejoin yarn to stitches on stitch holder (row 11), and work to match, reversing all shaping.

Back

Cast on 20 sts.

Work in st st, starting with a knit row.

Increase on next (that is, Row 3) and every following knit row until 54 sts.

Work 5 rows st st without shaping.

Decrease (use k2tog) at each end of every knit row until 46 sts.

Purl 1 row.

Row 1 K2tog, k21, turn and work on these stitches, leaving remaining stitches on a stitch holder.

Row 2 and every even row until row 16 Purl.

Row 3 K2tog, k18, k2tog. 20 sts.

Row 5 K2tog, knit to end. 19 sts.

Row 7 K2tog, k15, k2tog. 17 sts.

Row 9 K2tog, k13, k2tog. 15 sts.

Row 11 K2tog, k11, k2tog. 13 sts.

Row 13 K2tog, k9, k2tog. 11 sts.

Row 15 Bind off 2 sts, k6, k2tog. 8 sts.

Row 16 P2tog, p6. 7 sts.

Bind off remaining stitches.

With RS facing, rejoin yarn to stitches on stitch holder and work to match, reversing all shaping.

making up

Darn in any loose ends and press the work gently. Using the knitted pieces as a template, cut out two lining pieces, marking the opening in the front piece. Position the zipper to correspond with the opening in the front piece and pin into place, on the wrong side of the lining. Carefully slit the fabric to correspond with the zipper's teeth. Re-pin the lining, hemming it and slipstitching onto the zipper. Place the lining pieces right sides together and stitch. Take the knitted pieces and, wrong side together, stitch around the edges of the lip shape. You now have two sets of lips. Insert the lining lips into the knitted lips. Use some stuffing to 'pout out' the lips for a three-dimensional effect. Slipstitch the zipper to the edges of the knitted front.

tip Add a little extra love to this gift with the addition of a heart-shaped crocheted pull to the zipper. 3ch, ss into 1st st to create a loop, 2ch. Into loop work 1sc, 1dc, 1tr, 1dtr, 1tr, 1dc, 2sc, 1dtr, 2sc, 1tr, 1dtr, 1tr, 1dc, ss into loop and pull yarn tight. Work two heart shapes and stitch together. Plait all loose ends together and use to attach to the zipper. As an alternative, use a heart-shaped button or pendant.

tip When you have taken the time and trouble to make a gift for someone, give equal consideration to how it is presented. Present the lucky recipient with a taster of what lies within. Wrap the gift simply in white tissue paper and tie it not with ribbon but with a sample of the yarn used. in the pattern, finished off with a button tie or a jaunty feather.

Create a version of this purse in pink for a pretty, but still glitzy, alternative.

pooch
pullover

Treat your canine chum to a handmade dog jumper – just perfect for long autumn walks in the park.

Oh, to be a dog when the leaves begin to float from the trees at the end of a long summer. There is something remarkably satisfying about watching a small dog leap at falling russet-coloured leaves, with its seemingly endless capacity to spot a leaf, catch a leaf, spot a leaf, catch a leaf.

Rich red-hued autumnal foliage is what the colours in this red-and-orange-speckled yarn brought to mind to inspire this cute little dog jumper. It is knitted using a soft knitted linen-mix tape yarn. This is light-weight but quite chunky, and lends itself to producing more substantial items such as this autumn sweater. The jumper features simple shaping, with armholes (or should that be pawholes?) for your dog's front legs. There are no fastenings underneath; the jumper just covers the dog's back.

If you like your pet friends to be as well accessorized as you are, I have designed a simple leash to match the jumper – perfect for morning jaunts in the park. Just because it's before breakfast doesn't mean style should be neglected, after all.

The soft matte texture of this yarn is great for jumpers and coats – for humans too!

what you need and what you need to know...

yarns
2 x 1¾oz (50g) balls of bulky-weight (chunky) linen-mix tape yarn

needles
1 pair size 11 (8mm) needles

notions
Stitch holder

Darning needle

size
Suitable for a terrier or other small dog: round-the-body measurement will be about 12in (30cm); neck to hem measurement is 14in (35cm)

gauge
13 sts and 18 rows to 4in (10cm) square over garter stitch using size 11 (8mm) needles

pattern note This sweater has a garter-stitch border that is 4 stitches wide. The main pattern is a knit 4, purl 1 rib. When the pattern instructs you to 'inc 1', you need to maintain the k4, p1 pattern and knit or purl the increase stitch accordingly. For example, if you are on a right-side row, you will knit the first 4 stitches to maintain the garter-stitch border; then, if your next 4 stitches are 3 knit stitches and 1 purl, your increase stitch will be a knit stitch. The piece is knitted from the 'tail' end upwards, ending with a stretch ribbed collar.

This yarn has a lovely drape to it and will knit up satisfyingly quickly.

pattern
Cast on 24 sts.

Work 3 rows in garter stitch (knit every row).

Row 1 (RS) K4, k1, (p1, k4) 3 times, k4.

Row 2 (WS) K4, inc 1, (p4, k1) 3 times, p1, inc 1, k4. 26 sts.

These two rows set the pattern of keeping the first and last four stitches on every row as garter stitch throughout the pattern.

Row 3 K4, inc 1, k2, (p1, k4) 3 times, p1, inc 1, k4. 28 sts.

Row 4 K4, inc 1, p1, (k1, p4) 3 times, k1, p3, inc 1, k4. 30 sts.

Row 5 K4, inc 1 (k4, p1) 4 times, k2, inc 1, k4. 32 sts.

Row 6 K4, inc 1, p3, (k1, p4) 4 times, k1, inc 1, k4. 34 sts.

Row 7 K4, inc 1, k1 (p1, k4) 5 times, inc 1, k4. 36 sts.

Row 8 K4, inc 1, k1 (p4, k1) 5 times, p2, inc 1, k4. 38 sts.

Rows 9 and 10 Work across all sts, keeping patt correct.

Row 11 K4, inc 1, k3, (p1, k4) 5 times, p1, inc 1, k1, k4. 40 sts.

Row 12 Work across all sts, keeping patt correct.

Row 13 K4, inc 1, (k4, p1) 6 times, k2, inc 1, k4. 42 sts.

Work another 16 rows*, keeping patt correct.

Divide for paw holes
Row 30 (WS) K4, p3, k1 and turn. Working on these 8 sts only, work 12 rows** keeping patt correct. Break yarn and place these stitches on a stitch holder.

With WS facing, rejoin yarn to main knitting. Work across the middle 26 sts, turn and work on these sts only for 12 rows**. Break yarn and place these stitches on a stitch holder.

With WS facing, rejoin yarn to rem 8 sts and work in patt for 13 rows**.

Now work across all sts, working in patt for 8 rows***.

Next row K4, p2tog (p3, p2tog) 6 times, p2, k4. 35 sts.

Next row K4, (k2, k2tog) 6 times, k3, k4. 29 sts.

Next row K4, (k1, p1) to last 5 sts, k5. Work further 9 rows in this rib, keeping garter-stitch borders correct.

Bind off in rib patt.

making up
Darn in any loose ends. Place the piece right-side down. Cover with a damp cloth and press lightly with a hot iron. Fold the piece in half lengthways with the right sides together. Using mattress stitch, sew a seam to join the garter-stitch borders between the armholes, from the start to the end of the armholes. Don't make this seam too long, so the neckline is nice and loose.

tip It's quite easy to size up this pattern for a larger dog. The standard pullover will fit a pooch that measures around 12in (30cm) around the body. Measure your dog and for every 4in (10cm) extra, add in 5 extra stitches and work an additional rib into the pattern. The pattern will make a coat measuring 14in (35cm) from neck to hem. To increase the length, add in 4 additional rows at '*', 2 additional rows at '**', 4 additional rows at '***' and add a couple of extra rows on the collar.

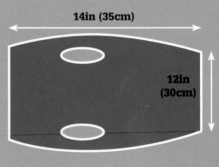

14in (35cm)

12in (30cm)

tip Why not design a coordinating leash to go with the pullover? This little leash is a shortie designed for fun rather than serious park pounding. You will need any left-over yarn from the pullover above, and a plastic or chrome leash attachment, which you should be able to buy at any hardware store. The leash is knitted wholly in garter stitch. Simply cast on 4 stitches and carry on knitting in garter stitch until you reach the right length for you, or you run out of your two balls, whichever comes first! When finished, fold over one end to create a hand-sized loop and stitch into place. Slip the other end through the leash hardware. Stitch firmly.

sassy stripe
armwarmers

These colourful armwarmers look fabulous when pushed around the wrists, just poking out from beneath a winter jacket.

Self-striping or self-patterning sock yarn is a marvellous invention. It offers the sock knitter the opportunity to make patterned and striped socks without fiddly yarn changing and complicated colour work. Some of my favourite self-patterning sock yarns are those that create Fair Isle-type patterns (see page 101). No one who knows what genuine Fair Isle looks like would mistake the marled, speckled and striped effect for the real thing, but the finished effect does hold its own. These wonderful yarns have reinvented the old knitting tradition of making hand-knitted socks for gifts – so much more special than buying a pair from a store!

Socks are traditionally knitted in the round using a set of four or five double-pointed needles rather than the standard two single-pointed needles (see page 20 for more instructions on this technique). This means you can knit a tube shape with no seams. Here, I've created a pattern to make a pair of mitten-style armwarmers. The longer length allows them to be pulled high, keeping wrists and arms warm, or pooled around the wrist – perfect for a friend who wants to keep looking stylish whatever the weather.

Self-striping yarn is a simple way to produce wonderful colour-changing effects.

what you need and what you need to know...

yarn
1 x 3½oz (100g) ball of variegated sock yarn

needles
Set of 4 size 2 (3mm) double-pointed needles

notions
Stitch holder
Darning needle

size
Because of the stretchy ribbing, the armwarmers will fit widthways in any size. Lucky people with long, elegant fingers may want to increase a few rows on the thumb shaping and the main hand shaping – about 8 extra rows should do. The armwarmers are about 14in (35cm) from end to fingertip.

gauge
24 sts and 36 rows to 4in (10cm) square over k2, p2 rib using size 2 (3mm) needles

pattern note The armwarmers are knitted from the bottom (the arm part) up to the fingers. They are made up of three tubes; stitches from the arm tube are taken to create two smaller tubes for the thumb and the hand.

Sock yarns generally have a high wool content, so will keep you cosily warm. They are also usually machine-washable so are easy to look after.

pattern

Make 2
Cast on 64 sts and divide these evenly between three of the needles and arrange them into a triangle. Place a marker to indicate the start of the round. Begin knitting in the round in k2, p2 rib, being careful not to twist the stitches. Work 82 rows in k2, p2 rib, ending with p2.

Start palm shaping
Round 1 M1p, k2, m1p, p2, (k2, p2) to end of round. 66 sts.
Round 2 P1, m1p, k2, m1p, p1 (k2, p2) to end. 68 sts.
Round 3 P2, k2, p4 (k2, p2) to end.
Round 4 M1k, p2, k2, p2, m1k, p2 (k2, p2) to end. 70 sts.
Round 5 K1, p2, k2, p2, k1, p2, (k2, p2) to end.
Round 6 M1k, k1, p2, k2, p2, m1k, k1, p2, (k2, p2) to end. 72 sts.
Round 7 (k2, p2) to end.
Round 8 (k2, p2) to end.
Round 9 K2, p2, k1, m1p, k1, p2, (k2, p2) to end. 73 sts.
Round 10 K2, p2, k1, p1, k1, p2, (k2, p2) to end.
Round 11 K2, p2, m1k, k1, p1, k1, m1k, p2, (k2, p2) to end. 75 sts.
Round 12 K2, p2, k2, p1, (k2, p2) to end.
Round 13 K2, p2, k2, p1, m1p, (k2, p2) to end. 76 sts.
Round 14 (k2, p2) to end.
Repeat this round 14 times more.

Shape thumb
Round 29 (k2, p2) to last 4 sts, k2, start next round 2 sts early.

Row 30 Inc 2k, (p2, k2) 4 times, p2, turn and work on these 20 sts only.
Next row Inc 2, (k2, p2) to end. Work straight on these 22 sts with no shaping for 24 rows.
Next row (p2tog, k2tog) 5 times, p2tog. 11 sts.
Cut the yarn, leaving a long piece of yarn (enough to sew up the thumb seam) and pull through remaining stitches using a darning needle. Pull tight and tie off.

Mitten section
Rejoin yarn to remaining stitches at the base of the new thumb piece. Work across body of the mitten. When you reach the thumb piece, inc 2 (60 sts). Work in the round with no shaping for 30 rounds. End last round so 2 new cast-on purl stitches are next.
Next round P2tog, (k2, p2) 7 times, k2tog, (p2, k2) 7 times. 58 sts.
Next round K2tog, k1, (p2, k2) 6 times, p2, p2tog, p1, (k2, p2) 6 times, k1, start next round 1 st early. 56 sts.
Next round K3tog, (p2, k2) 6 times, p1, p3tog, (k2, p2) 6 times. 52 sts.
Next round P3tog, p1, (k2, p2) 6 times, k2, p3tog, k1 (p2, k2) 6 times, p2. 48 sts.
Divide the remaining stitches onto two needles (24 sts each). Using the three-needle bind-off technique (see page 21), bind off 5 sts. There will be 19 sts left on each needle. Now patt 19 sts on one needle only. Turn the work and, again using the three-needle bind-off, bind off 5 sts. Again working off a single needle, patt to end. Then, for the last time, turn and bind off the remaining stitches.

tip Beware of creating ladders when knitting across four needles, because the first and last stitches on each needle can be knitted more loosely than the rest. An easy way to address this is to swap around the first and last couple of stitches across to the next needle every few rows.

making up

Darn in any loose ends. Place a damp cloth over the knitting and steam gently with an iron. Don't press too heavily, as you don't want to crush the ribbing. Use a darning needle to sew up the thumb seam.

tip Sock yarn is, of course, perfect for producing socks (well, the clue is in the name). However, you can also use sock yarn to create any tubey item — leggings, boob tubes and cowl necks could all be easily produced in the trademark patterns and stripes with no fiddly yarn changing.

The intricate patterns and colour changes of traditional Fair Isle knitting can be reproduced with much less fiddly work by using self-patterning sock yarn.

gilt-edged
glitter belt

This glamorous gold-edged belt makes the perfect gift for a friend who knows how to make an impact with stylish accessories.

Ribbon yarns aren't all about slippery, satiny surfaces. Some types of this yarn also capture the joy of fuzzy mohair or angora to create an extremely soft, flat yarn with the luminosity of a ribbon. Such creations are great examples of gourmet yarn. These yarns tend to be slight and come in small packages with a hefty price tag to match the exquisite colourways. They are the complete opposite from the chunky, handmade dip-dyed yarns that look as if they have been shorn from the sheep, dipped into dye and hung on a peg to dry in the wind. Instead, these ethereal ribbons look as if they could have been crafted by fairies.

The pattern for this chic crocheted belt matches an especially delicate, wispy ribbon yarn with a more crisp and hardy gold-coloured lurex yarn. The yarns are used both singly and together: this creates three different effects. The belt is made from a series of small and large crocheted rounds. The rounds are joined together with simple slip stitches and finished with a pretty gold shell edging. To ramp up the glamorous effect, the belt tie is embellished with lengths of sparkling beads.

The sheen of this satiny ribbon yarn enhances the beautifully subtle colourway.

what you need and what you need to know...

yarn
1 x 1¾oz (50g) ball light-weight (DK) nylon and mohair mix ribbon

1 x ⅞oz (25g) ball of fine-weight (4ply) lurex

hook
7 (4.5 mm)

notions
Darning needle

Selection of beads and jewellery chain

12in (30cm) piece of felt in a toning colour

Iron-on webbing

size
This is a hipster belt that will fit any size. If you want to make it a little more generous, simply make an extra round or two (you won't need any extra balls of yarn) and add in to the row of larger roundels across the back. The small roundels are 2¼–2¾in (6–7cm) wide; the larger roundels are about 4in (10cm) in diameter.

gauge
Achieving an exact gauge is not essential for this project.

pattern note In this pattern, tr denotes an American treble. Those used to British patterns should instead do a British double treble (see pages 15 and 23).

pattern

Small roundels (make 4)
Using both ribbon and lurex yarns held together, make 4 ch and join with a ss in first ch to make a ring.

Round 1 3 ch (counts as first dc), 11 dc into ring, 1 ss into 3rd ch of first 3 ch, 3 ch, turn.

Round 2 1 dc in same place as ss, 2 dc in each dc, 1 ss into 3rd ch of first 3 ch. Pull yarn through and cut.

Large roundels (make 6)
Using ribbon yarn only, follow pattern as for small roundel; at end of Round 2, instead of cutting yarn: 3 ch, turn.

Round 3 1 dc in same place as ss, (1 dc in next dc, 2 dc in next 2 dc) to last 2 dc, 1 dc in each of last, 1 ss into 3rd ch of first 3 ch. Pull yarn through and cut.

making up
Press pieces gently using a damp cloth and a warm iron. Lay out the pieces in the following order (S = small; L = large):

S L S L L L L S L S

Pin each roundel to its neighbouring piece at the place where they meet on the curve. Working in the lurex yarn and starting in the middle of a far-edge curve of an outer round, work a chain of gold slip stitches around the front edge of the circle, joining each roundel to the next one with a slip stitch when they meet. Work across the top of all the roundels, joining the pieces as you go, and then work along the bottom edge on the way back. Without cutting the yarn, continue to go around the first two rounds again (one small, one large) in a shell pattern (miss a st, 5 dc into next st, miss a st, ss). Work all the way around the curves, adding a hdc across the ss joining the rounds together. With the large round, it looks nice if you can work the shell edging from the top of the rounds, leaving a slight gap between the gold chain stitch already worked and the new shell pattern.

Yarns with such a gentle touch as this ribbon yarn lend themselves to fragile wraps, scarves and sweaters with delicate buttons and lace fringing.

tip The belt can be fastened with a simple ribbon tie, but I think that this kind of hip belt looks lovely with a bit of a flourish. For the tie shown here, attach four strands of lurex yarn to each small edging roundel and work a chain as long as you need – about 6in (15cm) should be enough. Then add weight to the tie with the addition of a beaded cluster (I used an old necklace, cut into two beaded pieces), a heavy pendant, or even a pretty pebble with a handy hole in it.

tip The belt is quite delicate, especially the larger roundels made in the lighter ribbon only, so it's a good idea to give it a little substance. Take a piece of toning felt and cut to the size of the large rounds. Cut four rounds to fit across the back four pieces. Use an iron-on interfacing to iron the two pieces together. Follow the directions on the pack, although I would recommend ironing the pieces together with a damp cloth between the iron and the work. Trim the felt pieces to size.

bollywood
bag

This fabulously vibrant furry bag would make a beautiful gift for a fiery and outgoing friend.

When I spotted this crazy-looking yarn, I bought it on impulse with no idea of what I was going to make. It is very soft and the colour is multi-tonal, which gives this particular shade of red real depth. Eventually, after living with balls of this lovely yarn and stroking them like some kind of substitute pet, Diwali (the Hindu Festival of Lights) came. The colour and brightness of the yarn reminded me of the fireworks celebrating the festival, and so the Bollywood bag was born. Such yarns have most impact when used in small amounts, and I thought a bag would show it off best. A jumper made in this yarn would make the wearer look like a grizzly bear, or, in this vibrant yarn, like a very furry alien.

The bag is made in two triangle shapes. The back piece is knitted with an additional flap which hangs down the front of the bag to keep it closed. When using a yarn like this, a simple shape tends to work best. For any of these furry yarns there is no point using fancy stitches, as they are completely lost behind the tufts and fluffs. As if it weren't extravagant-looking enough, the bag is also trimmed with beads and pom poms.

The filaments of silky and metallic thread make this yarn extremely tactile.

what you need and what you need to know...

yarn
2 x 1¾oz (50g) balls of light-weight (DK) novelty yarn with wisps and fibres

needles
1 pair size 5 (3.75mm) needles

notions
Darning needle

20in (50cm) toning fabric for lining

Long necklace in toning colour to make handle, or gold chain or a selection of beads

4 small pom poms (optional)

Sewing kit for hand sewing or sewing machine

size
8 by 10½in (20 by 27cm) at widest and longest points

gauge
24 sts and 30 rows to 4in (10cm) square over garter stitch using size 5 (3.75mm) needles

These eye-catching yarns are best used as punctuation – cuffs, scarves, bags or edgings – rather than complete outfits.

pattern

Front
Cast on 41 sts.

Knit 40 rows garter stitch (every row knit).

Row 41 K2tog, knit to last 2 sts, k2tog. 39 sts.

Knit a further 4 rows.

Row 46 K2tog, knit to last 2 sts, k2tog. 37 sts.

Knit a further 4 rows.

Row 51 K2tog, knit to last 2 sts, k2tog. 35 sts.

Knit a further 4 rows.

Row 56 K2tog, knit to last 2 sts, k2tog. 33 sts.

Knit a further 2 rows.

Repeat these last 3 rows 14 times. 5 sts.

Row 101 K2tog, K1, K2tog. 3 sts.

Cast off rem 3 sts.

Back (starting with flap)
Cast on 3 sts.

Knit 1 row.

Row 2 Inc 1, knit to end, inc 1. 5 sts.

Knit a further 2 rows.

Rep these last 3 rows 19 times. 41 sts. This completes the flap.

Cont the back as for front piece.

making up

Darn in any loose ends. Place the knitted pieces under a damp cloth and steam the knitting gently with an iron. Using each knitted piece as a template, cut two pieces of lining. Sew the sides of the lining together and then slipstitch the hems to the knitted piece on the front edge and around the flap's point. Sew the knitted pieces together.

Measure the length of your desired handle. I chose a handle long enough to allow the bag to be held by hand, or tucked under the arm over the shoulder. A long chain to hang across the body would work well, as would a very shallow handle. If using a chain handle or ready-made beaded necklace, use the hooks to sew onto the bag, or thread contrasting beads onto double lengths of strong embroidery thread and create your own necklace to use as a handle. Sew on securely, darning in any loose ends.

Create three beaded lengths, with optional pom pom ends, and attach to the point of the flap securely. Hide the 'sewing on' with a further pom pom or glass bead. These beaded lengths are decorative, but also weight the flap down to keep the bag closed and safe.

tip If your lifestyle is more Hollywood than Bollywood, this pattern would look very red-carpet fabulous knitted in black yarn with gold metallic highlights, complete with a golden chain handle.

yarns used

Below is a list of the yarns that we used to make the projects in the book, should you want to recreate them exactly. I have given the approximate yardage of each yarn so you can substitute with your own choice of yarn as you like. To work out how much substitute yarn you will need, make this simple calculation:

- **Multiply the number of balls of the recommended yarn by the number of yards/metres per ball = A**
- **The number of yards/metres per ball of your replacement yarn = B**
- **The number of balls of replacement yarn you require = A ÷ B**

page 25 Home

Page 26 Warm-hearted bedwarmer
Lilac version: 2 x 1¾oz (50g) balls of Karabella Brushed Alpaca (100% alpaca – 35yd/32m per ball) in shade 1074 (Lavender).
Pink version: 2 x 1¾oz (50g) balls of Lana Grossa Caldo (100% wool – 38yd/35m per ball) in shade 64.

Page 30 Pebble pillows
Small pillow: 2 x 3½oz (100g) balls of Rowan Spray (100% wool – 87yd/80m per ball) in shade 007 (Calm).

Large pillow: 2 x 3½oz (100g) balls of Rowan Spray (100% wool – 87yd/80m per ball) in shade 002 (Mellow).

Page 34 Rainbow rags storage cube
2 x 1¾oz (50g) balls of Tahki Yarns Poppy (45% nylon, 28% cotton, 27% acrylic – 81yd/74m per ball) in shade 04.

Page 38 Fruit fizz coasters
Rowan Cotton Glace (100% cotton – 125yd/115m per 1¾oz/50g ball) in shades 820 (Pick & Mix), 814 (Shoot) and 739 (Dijon). Jaeger Siena 4 ply (100% mercerized cotton 153yd/140m per 1¾oz/50g ball) in shades 420 (Buttermilk) and 412 (Sapling).

Page 42 Bubbles & bobbles cushion
2 x 3½oz (100g) balls of Adriafil Set Trends Art (94% wool, 6% nylon – 33yd/30m per ball) in shade 50.

page 45 Kids

Page 46 Fun-fur baby bonnet
Girl's bonnet: A 1 x 1¾oz (50g) ball of Jaeger Baby Merino DK (100% merino wool – 131yd/120m per ball) in shade 193 (Yo Yo); B 1 x 1¾oz (50g) ball of Jaeger Fur (47% kid mohair, 47% wool, 6% polyamide – 22yd/20m per ball) in shade 056 (Moose).

Boy's bonnet: A 1 x 1¾oz (50g) ball of Jaeger Baby Merino DK (100% merino wool – 131yd/120m per ball) in shade 191 (Pogo); B 1 x 1¾oz (50g) ball of Jaeger Fur (47% kid mohair, 47% wool, 6% polyamide – 22yd/20m per ball) in shade 050 (Bear).

Page 50 Knitty kitty backpack

Backpack: 2 x 1¾oz (50g) balls of Karabella Labirinth (57% merino wool, 12% superkid mohair, 17% nylon, 14% acrylic – 81yd/74m per ball) in shade 305.

Pyjama case: 2 1¾oz (50g) balls of Debbie Bliss Cashmerino Astrakhan (10% cashmere, 60% merino wool, 30% microfibre – 76yd/69m per ball) in shades 004 (Chocolate) and 007 (Yellow).

Page 56 Super-soft slippers

Rowan Kidsilk Haze (70% superkid mohair, 30% silk – 229yd/210m per ⅞oz/25g ball) in shades 590 (Pearl), 592 (Heavenly) and 606 (Candy Girl). Rowan Kid Classic (70% lambswool, 26% kid mohair, 4% nylon – 151yd/140m per 1¾oz/50g ball) in shades 842 (Peach Sorbet and 822 (Glacier).

Page 60 Colourful capelet

2 x 3½oz (100g) balls of Rowan Chunky Print (100% wool – 109yd/100m per ball in shade 077 (Girlie Pink). Pom-poms were made using Jaeger Baby Merino DK (100% merino wool –

131yd/120m per 1¾oz/50g ball) in various shades.

Page 64 Giddy gilet

2 x 1¾oz (50g) Lanartus Aloha (23% wool, 38% polyamide, 37% polyester, 2% metallic polyester – 38yd/35m per ball) in shade 4557 (Graphite) and 4561 (Reds).

Page 67 Adults

Page 68 Running river ribbon scarf

Blue scarf: 2 x 1¾ oz (50g) balls of Knit One, Crochet Too Tartelette (50% cotton, 50% nylon – 75yd/68m per ball) in shade 630 (Blueberry).

Red scarf: 2 x 1¾oz (50g) balls of Louisa Harding Sari Ribbon (90% polyamide, 10% metallic – 66yd/60m per ball) in shade 03.

Page 72 Simple slub shrug

2 x 3½oz (100g) balls of Colinette Graffiti (100% wool – 87yd/80m per ball) in shade 143 (Peaches and Cream).

Page 76 Corsage camisole

2 x 1¾oz (50g) balls of Rowan Cotton Tape (100% cotton – 72yd/67m per ball) in shade 550 (Electric).

Page 80 Two-tone twist scarf

Main project: 2 x 3½oz (100g) skeins of Noro Transitions (55% wool, 10% silk, 7% cashmere, 7% angora, 7% alpaca, 7% kid mohair, 7% camel – 132yd/120m per ball) in shades 06 and 04.

Variation: 1 x 3½oz (100g) ball of Debbie Bliss Maya (100% wool – 137yd/126m per ball) in shade 08 and 2 x 1¾oz (50g) balls of Debbie Bliss Cashmerino Aran (55% merino, 33% microfibre, 12% cashmere – 98yd/90m per ball) in shade 012 (Mauve).

Page 84 Classic cloche hat

Pink hat: 2 x 1¾oz (50g) balls of Rowan Cotton Braid (68% cotton, 22% viscose, 10% linen – 46yd/50m per ball) in shade 351 (Monet).

Green hat: 2 x 1¾oz (50g) balls of Rowan Cotton Braid (68% cotton, 22% viscose, 10% linen – 46yd/50m per ball) in shade 353 (Renoir).

Page 89 Gifts

Page 90 Pucker-up purse

Red purse: 2 x 1¾oz (50g) balls of Twilleys Goldfingering (80% viscose, 20% metallized polyester – 218yd/200m per ball) in shade 38 (Red).

Pink purse: 2 x ⅞oz (25g) balls of Rowan Lurex Shimmer (80% viscose, 20% polyester – 103yd/95m per ball) in shade 336 (Gleam).

Pooch pullover

2 x 1¾oz (50g) balls of Rowan Linen Print (70% viscose, 30% linen 50yd/55m per ball) in shade 342 (Blush).

Page 98 Sassy stripe armwarmers

1 x 3½oz (100g) ball of Opal Rainforest Sock Yarn (75% wool, 25% polymide – 465yd/425m per ball) in shade RF4 (Flamingo).

Page 102 Gilt-edged glitter belt

1 x 1¾oz (50g) ball of Louisa Harding Impression (84% nylon, 16% fine kid mohair – 154yd/140m per ball) in colour 04; 1 x ⅞oz (25g) ball of Rowan Lurex Shimmer (80% viscose, 20% polyester – 103yd/95m per ball) in shade 332 (Gold).

Page 106 Bollywood bag

2 x 1¾oz (50g) balls of Wendy Chic (60% nylon, 30% polyester, 10% metallized polyester – 87yd/80m per ball) in shade 251 (Raphael).

suppliers

Recommended yarn stores

Every craftster has their favourite yarn store, where they know they can get advice and have a chat about a challenging project. My two favourites are:

Purl
137 Sullivan Street
New York
NY 10012
Tel 212 420 8796
www.purlsoho.com
This knitting boutique in Soho also has a fabulous online shop selling books and magazines as well as yarns.

Loop
41 Cross Street
Islington
London
N1 2BB
Tel (+44) 020 72881160
www.loop.gb.com
This is a small but beautiful knit salon stocking yarns, needles and knitted items from a small band of designers. It is well worth a visit if you are in London for its friendly advice and loyalty card scheme.

Recommended online stores

You could also try a little online searching to find yarns that are extra-special and may not be stocked in every yarn store in every town. Here are a few of the best online stores (in my opinion); they have a wide range, carry enough stock so you don't have to wait long to receive your order, and have sites that are easy to navigate:

www.angelyarns.com
www.yarncountry.com
www.yarnmarket.com

Yarn manufacturers

Yarns used in the projects in this book were made by the following manufacturers:

Adriafil
www.adriafil.com
Colinette
www.colinette.com
Debbie Bliss
www.designeryarns.uk.com
Karabella
www.karabellayarns.com
Knit One, Crochet Too
www.knitonecrochettoo.com
Lana Grosso
www.lanagrossa.com
Lanartus
www.yarnmarket.com
Louisa Harding
www.designeryarns.uk.com
Noro
www.eisakunoro.com
Opal
www.angelyarns.com
Rowan
www.knitrowan.com
RYC
www.ryclassic.com
Tahki
www.tahkistacycharles.com
Wendy
www.tbramsden.co.uk

Buttons and trimmings

When you need buttons, beads and trimmings to create the perfect finishing touch for your latest knitted or crocheted creation, try these stockists:

Buttontiques
www.2camtech.com/buttontiques/forgetme.html
I love this website, which is run by a real button enthusiast based in the US. The owner calls buttons 'art in miniature'.

The Button Queen
19 Marylebone Lane
London W1V 2NF
Tel +44 20 7935 1505
www.thebuttonqueen.co.uk
In the heart of London's West End, The Button Queen is dedicated to antique and modern buttons. It is a treasure trove for anyone interested in embellishments to finish off a hand-knitted or crafted piece. Do try to visit if you are in London, or, if you ask nicely, they will post items anywhere in the world.

VV Rouleaux
54 Sloane Square
Cliveden Place
London
SW1W 8AW
Tel (+44) 020 7730 3125
www.vvrouleaux.com
This shop is a mecca for anyone who likes trimmings; it stocks ribbons, feathers, fringes and appliqué. As well as having a chain of shops across the UK, it also offers a mail-order service.

index

about the author

Jenny Hill has successfully been running Small Acorns, a company specializing in knitting and crochet for babies and children, for five years. Jenny lives in Bradworthy, Devon.